TINA TOWNER

My story as the youngest photographer at the Kennedy assassination

TINA TOWNER PENDER

Copyright © 2012
All rights reserved.

ISBN: 1466287128
ISBN 13: 9781466287129

Library of Congress Control Number: 2011915792
CreateSpace Independent Publishing Platform
North Charleston, South Carolina

*In memory of my loving parents,
James M. and Patricia D. Towner,
who dedicated their lives to each other and
to their three daughters who love them beyond description.
May they rest in peace.*

Dedications

*To my sons Scott, Chris and daughter Carley and their families
and to my sisters Nancy and Patsy and their families.
I love you so very much, and I am thankful you are in my life.*

And

*To my dear husband Gene,
whom I cannot thank enough for encouraging
me to tell my story and for giving me the opportunity to
do so. I could not and would not have been able to
do this without you in my life.
I love you.*

Contents

Acknowledgement ix

Introduction xi

Chapter 1 *A Little Family History* 1

Chapter 2 *1963, President Kennedy Comes to Dallas* 3

Chapter 3 *The Rest of the '60s* 39

Chapter 4 *1970–1979, The Postal Connection* 47

Chapter 5 *1980–1989, The Sixth Floor Exhibit* 53

Chapter 6 *1990–1999, The Photographers Gather* 59

Chapter 7 *2000–2009, A Whole Other Life* 65

Chapter 8 *2010 Forward, Gearing Up* 71

Chapter 9 *Where Were You?* 79

Epilogue 83

Sources 93

Other Sources 95

Acknowledgement

I would like to thank Gary Mack, curator of the Sixth Floor Museum at Dealey Plaza in Dallas, Texas, for his continued support since I first spoke with him in 1980. Even before Gary joined the Museum as archivist in 1994, he was a tremendous advocate for my parents and me, and he continued to show a sincere interest in my family and in our JFK materials.

After Gary joined the Museum, my family's relationship with Gary broadened into a similar relationship with the entire Sixth Floor organization. Therefore, I wish to express my sincere appreciation to The Sixth Floor Museum at Dealey Plaza and everyone associated with it for his or her help, support, and patience over the years.

Thank you. Thank you. Thank you.

Introduction

On November 22, 1963, I was an eyewitness to the John F. Kennedy assassination. I stood with my parents James M. and Patricia D. Towner in Dealey Plaza on the southwest corner of Elm and Houston streets, directly across Elm Street from the Texas School Book Depository building. My parents were fifty years old. I was thirteen and, as far as I know, the youngest photographer at that tragic event.

At the site that day, my father took a total of four color transparencies using a Yashica 44 twin lens camera. At the same time he was photographing the presidential limousine, I was taking 8 mm color home movies with a Sears Tower Varizoom movie camera. Daddy taught me how to use the movie camera as soon as we got it, so I was experienced with handling it. He also showed me how to use the Yashica twin lens and explained to me all of its intricacies, but I didn't use it much unless he preset it for me and all I had to do was focus, aim and snap. The first of Daddy's four photos is of the presidential limousine as it turned the corner around us. This remarkable historic photograph, originally a color image, is (as of 2012) prominently displayed in black and white in The Sixth Floor Museum at Dealey Plaza, which I will also refer to as The Sixth Floor Exhibit, the Exhibit, The Sixth Floor Museum, or the Museum. (The Sixth Floor Museum at Dealey Plaza opened its doors in 1989 under the name of The Sixth Floor Exhibit. The name was officially changed to The Sixth Floor Museum in the mid-1990s, and in 1997, it became The Sixth Floor Museum at Dealey Plaza.) One of the Museum's exhibits is a list of eyewitnesses and a diagram of where each eyewitness stood that day. Because my parents and I were never officially interviewed, this exhibit does not mention our names.

When my father died in 2002, he had accumulated very little documentation about the assassination. I doubt much came past him. I have a few objects of memorabilia, including magazines, newspapers, books, video tapes, and CDs, but most of my collection consists of correspondence. Since November 22, 1963, I have kept almost all the letters I have written and received pertaining to the assassination, and I have made numerous notes to the files. I keep all of the documentation in volumes of three-ring binders. I store items not suitable for a three-ring binder in plastic storage boxes. My father saved most of the few letters from *Life* magazine and *'Teen* magazine, but there were very few other documents in his files. Knowing how much my father liked to write and how much he did write with a flourish about his childhood, military background, family life, family vacations, and his and Mother's rock hunting excursions, I am surprised that he wrote nothing about November 22, 1963. It must have been too painful for him. I so wish that he had recorded his thoughts and feelings about the assassination while they were still relatively fresh on his mind. On the other hand, I wonder if I would have written anything about the subject up until now if *'Teen* magazine had not asked me to write my story in 1968, for I had not written anything down until that time. It is a good thing they contacted me.

As a young adult, I once told my father I would like to write a book someday. I told him I didn't know what I would write about, but it was something I would like to do. I was not thinking about the Kennedy assassination when I said that. I was referring to nothing in particular. Daddy replied that I had to live long enough to have something to write about. Little did I know that my first book would be about something that had already happened to me when I made that statement. Daddy was a rock hound and wrote numerous articles for *Lapidary Journal* about his and Mother's many rock-hunting adventures. When

Introduction

I made my declaration about writing, I did not know he took a correspondence writing course in the 1970s and kept a journal for a number of years—something he never mentioned to me. I was aware of his writing for *Lapidary Journal*, but I did not learn about the correspondence course until I went through his files after he and Mother entered a nursing home in 2002.

As far as my having something to write about, until 2009 it never occurred to me that I might actually have something of interest to say about being a teenage amateur photographer at the site of the Kennedy assassination. I never felt I had much of a story and thought many times that my claim to fame is, having been a witness to this historical event, I still somehow had no story.

Until recently, I had not thought much about why I felt my story was insignificant. It probably has a lot to do with how what I witnessed and recorded on film compares to the eyewitness accounts of people who were closer to the president than I was when he was shot. Immediately following the assassination, and for decades to follow, Abraham Zapruder's film was almost all anyone talked about. His film was "the evidence" that mattered most to the authorities, to the media, and to the public. A few other amateur photographers who captured the presidential limousine at the time of the fatal gunshot or people who witnessed the fatal head wound also attracted attention. My eyewitness account seemed comparatively insignificant; so when people asked me what I saw, in comparison to the close eyewitnesses, my answers were a letdown. After all, I *was* standing right there; I *must* have seen something. All of these things considered, answering questions has been awkward, so I have been content to stay in the background.

In my presence, someone once asked Gary Mack, curator of The Sixth Floor Museum at Dealey Plaza, what my story was, and he replied, "Tina's story is that she doesn't have one." He put into words exactly how I felt, and it was true up to a point. The answer to "Did you see President Kennedy get shot?"—no. The answer to "What did you hear?"—three shots. I don't think these are the answers people are hoping for. They aren't provocative enough. My answers are, more accurately, that I saw a lot, I heard a lot, and I felt a lot.

My good friend Kaye Lotman has taken a big interest in my story. Immediately after watching a 2009 National Geographic documentary, which included my film, she telephoned me and asked me a stream of questions, commenting that she could come up with many more questions if I wanted her to. She believed many people would be interested in what I have to say. The questions she asked me at that time were very different from the few, but usual, questions others have asked me in the past. Many of her questions were about feelings, not facts, and I began to realize that perhaps I did have something to write about. Thank you, Kaye, for inspiring me to begin this project by asking me such insightful and thought-provoking questions.

Readers will find no new evidence between the covers of this book that will help solve one of the world's biggest mysteries. I wrote my story mostly to document events in my life pertaining to the Kennedy assassination, but maybe some people will come away with a better idea of what it must feel like to have witnessed this historic event.

In one of Daddy's journals, he wrote about his first published article in a 1968 issue of *Lapidary Journal*. He said the acceptance and publication of his story was a very satisfying experience, but he felt like he should conceal how happy he was about it. He wrote that he wasn't really ashamed that he had written a rock-hound story, but he was humbled that *Lapidary Journal* would use it, and perhaps it was just beginners luck or maybe it was an oversight by the magazine editor. Over the next twenty-three years, he went on to write over thirty-seven articles for *Lapidary Journal* and a few articles for *Rockhound* and *Gems and Minerals* magazines. Publishing his stories was definitely not an oversight by the editor. Daddy must have been very satisfied with his writing success, and I am sorry I didn't take a bigger interest in them when he wrote them.

I compare how Daddy felt about publishing his first magazine article to the way I feel about publishing this, my first book. However, with my ability to self-publish, I do not have to concern myself with a publisher's approval, so like it or not, here it comes. My journey began on December 26, 2009—my mother's birthday. She would have been 97.

CHAPTER 1

A Little Family History

My father James Madsen Towner was former military. He enrolled in ROTC at Kansas State College, where he graduated in 1938 with a BS in Civil Engineering. He wanted to take geology at Kansas State, but they didn't offer it. Instead, the school advisor encouraged him to become a Civil Engineer. He and Mother met at Kansas State and married in 1935. Daddy entered the US Army on September 11, 1941. In 1942, he was stationed at Drew Field in Orlando, Florida. He acquired the temporary rank of lieutenant colonel and remained in Florida until they discharged him in 1946 with the permanent rank of major. He was an expert marksman and carried a camera with him in the swamps of Florida.

Mother was a homemaker. She never worked outside the home, but she worked hard inside the home. She and Daddy were dedicated to each other and to my sisters Patsy and Nancy and me. They were loving, affectionate, and attentive parents. Mother played the piano beautifully, and my sisters and I looked forward to hearing her beautiful music wafting through the open windows and down the street as we walked home from school every day—literally music to our ears. Mother suffered from early onset of macular degeneration and began to go blind when I was in high school, but she never complained.

Daddy bought his first camper trailer in 1956 and took the family on vacations every summer, mostly to the Rocky Mountains. Since Daddy and Mother were avid rock-hounds (especially Daddy), our trips always included rock hunts. He also cut, polished, or faceted his precious and semi-precious stones until he couldn't sit upright any longer. He even took his faceting machine into the nursing home with him, which was a comfort to him; although I don't think he ever used it. He was a talented artist, and he did some beautiful work with his gemstones until his body began to fail him.

I was born and raised in Oak Cliff in Dallas, Texas. My parents and my two older sisters, Nancy and Patsy, moved to Oak Cliff in 1946, four years before I was born. By the time I came along, Daddy was working in the steel business, selling steel to contractors, and he never had a job he liked. I attended George Peabody elementary school in the first through sixth grades. In 1962, we moved to another area of Oak Cliff, and I attended seventh grade at John W. Carpenter elementary school. I attended T. W. Browne Junior High and Justin F. Kimball High School (that's right—JFK). I graduated from Kimball High School in 1968 and enrolled as a freshman at Texas Technological College (now a university) in Lubbock, Texas, where I attended one year. I left home in late summer 1969 when I married my college sweetheart. With an empty nest, Mother and Dad continued to live in Oak Cliff until 1972 when they moved to Hamilton, Texas, where Daddy took his final job at Hamilton Steel before he retired.

My oldest sister Patsy told me that before I was born Mother and Dad took her and Nancy to see President Truman when he drove down Davis Street in Oak Cliff sometime around 1947 or 1948. Patsy said she was about seven or eight years old at the time. I learned this while writing this book, and, certainly, Daddy's wanting to take me to see President Kennedy followed logically with his interest in taking my sisters to see President Truman.

CHAPTER 2

1963
President Kennedy
Comes to Dallas

In October 1963, Daddy read an article in the local newspaper reporting President Kennedy's scheduled trip to Dallas in November. I don't know if Daddy voted for Kennedy, but he seemed to like him OK, and I think he would have wanted to go see the presidential motorcade, regardless of who the president was. I knew nothing about politics and only read the newspaper when required to by a teacher as a school assignment, but I did know who President Kennedy was. On a humorous note, my parents thought it was cute how I tried (rather pathetically, in my opinion) to imitate Kennedy's voice, which they asked me to do often for family entertainment.

I probably wasn't as enthused about the president's visit as my parents would have liked me to be, but a week or two before the president's scheduled trip to Dallas, Daddy asked me if I wanted to get out of school to go with him and Mother to see the presidential motorcade. I jumped at the chance. I assume they were doing this primarily for me, but maybe they would have gone without me.

Prior to the scheduled motorcade, a public announcement indicated that going to see the presidential motorcade would be an excused absence from public school. Maybe T. W. Browne Junior High was the only school allowing this, but I believe it was the entire Dallas Independent School District. I was in the eighth grade. My mother wrote an excuse for me to give to the school's attendance office, and my parents picked me up from school around 9:30 or 10:00 a.m. I heard there were a few other students doing the same thing, but I didn't know any of them by name. My parents allowed me to invite a couple of my friends to go with us that day, but they were not able to go.

Friday, November 22, 1963, was a pretty day. It was partly cloudy and cool. Some reports said it was a warm and sunny fall day, but it was cool enough for me to wear my blue sweater, which is visible in some photographs taken by other amateur photographers at the site. We drove from Oak Cliff across the Houston Street viaduct toward downtown Dallas, only six or seven miles from our house. Daddy had already decided where he wanted to go to watch the motorcade. He thought the best place would be at the end of the motorcade route, at or near the Elm and Houston intersection. He believed it would be less crowded there, parking would be free at the nearby Union Terminal, and we could walk to the site from our car. After turning the corner onto Elm from Houston and passing by the grassy knoll area, the motorcade would disappear under the triple underpass, enter Stemmons Freeway, and head toward its next stop at the Dallas Trade Mart for a luncheon where President Kennedy was scheduled to speak.

In 1963, Union Terminal was a very busy train terminal located where Union Station is today. We parked in a large parking lot on the west side of the terminal and walked through Union Terminal, which smelled heavily of exhaust fumes. We continued walking north on Houston to the corner of Houston and Elm. From our car, the walk through the parking lot and train terminal was at least a couple of blocks. It was then approximately another four blocks to Elm Street.

We arrived at our chosen spot early, around 11:00 a.m. The motorcade was scheduled to arrive around 12:30 p.m. Daddy said his first choice for a good vantage point was on Elm Street about halfway down the hill from Houston toward the triple underpass. He thought that location would allow us a clear view of Kennedy's motorcade as it came down the hill from Houston, and he would have more time to focus the camera. However, I began to feel queasy standing in the sun, so we stayed up on the plaza where there was a little shade that Mother and I could sit in while we waited. We picked our spot on the corner; but Daddy still wanted to check out the area farther down the hill to make sure there wasn't a better location for us. He decided we could stay where we were, and we planted ourselves on the southwest corner of Elm and Houston, directly across Elm from the Texas School Book Depository building. While we waited, Mother and I took turns sitting on a small, green, folding camping stool we brought with us for that purpose. Like most of the men that day, Daddy was dressed in a suit and tie; Mother and I were each in a sweater and skirt, and I was wearing bobby sox and flats.

As we waited for the motorcade, I recall that Daddy looked up at the buildings on "our" corner and observed a number of people looking out of the windows. He commented that they really had birds' eye views and specifically mentioned watching one woman lean out of the window in a building catercorner to the Texas School Book Depository building. In our oral history recorded by the Museum in March 1996, Daddy stated that most of the windows in the TSBD had the shades pulled down. He also stated, as he had stated several times over the years to family and friends, that he told a uniformed police officer standing next to him that he saw a man in a white coat standing in a sixth floor window. Several times over the decades, Daddy repeated that the police officer saw this person, too.

While we were waiting for the motorcade, some excitement erupted nearby when someone was either sick or hurt and an ambulance came.

This happened on Houston between Main and Elm Streets. Daddy said we were standing about fifty feet from this commotion, which didn't seem to last long. It cleared up quickly. I am still not sure what happened.

As the motorcade finally approached, Daddy, Mother, and I took positions next to each other on the corner around which the motorcade would turn. Daddy asked a uniformed police officer for permission to step off the curb (which has since been removed to comply with the Americans with Disabilities Act), and we stepped into the street in order to better photograph the president when he came by. Standing to my left, almost elbow to elbow with me but a step behind, Daddy opened the viewfinder on the top of his Yashica camera, pushed the magnifier out of the way, held the camera up to his face, looked through the hole in the viewfinder, and captured one magnificent color photograph of the presidential limousine. At the same time, I took 8 mm movies with the Sears Tower Varizoom movie camera. With her arms folded and her purse looped over her arm, Mother stood a step or two behind me and to my right and watched the motorcade. I looked through the viewfinder, as Daddy taught me to do, and smoothly panned the camera in motion with the limousine, as it turned left onto Elm directly in front of and around me. Jackie appeared to be looking right at me. In no way did I understand the enormity of even that moment, not to mention the tragedy only seconds away. Because of the obtuse angle of the Houston and Elm corner, the presidential limo began to disappear down the hill into the crowd to my left. I continued filming until I could see only the back of the limousine. The meter on the movie camera was broken, which we were already aware of, and Daddy told me earlier that I would know when the film ran out when I heard the clicking sound of the film inside the camera. He knew before we left home that the reel of film in the movie camera was nearing the end; however, he was confident I would have plenty of film for what I needed. Under expected circumstances, this would have been true.

After the limo passed us by, bystanders on our corner began to move back up onto the curb, and many of them turned and started following the president's limo down the hill. Both of my parents began to walk away from where I continued filming a few seconds longer. The Zapruder film shows a little girl with a scarf on her head running down the hill along Elm following the presidential motorcade. I have been asked if I am that little girl. I am not.

Elsie Dorman was filming the motorcade from the fourth floor of the Texas School Book Depository. She was not looking through her viewfinder much of the time, so she actually captured more of the Towner family than she did the motorcade. Her historic JFK film clearly shows the three of us as Daddy and I photograph the limousine turning in front of us onto Elm. Daddy completes taking his photograph, lowers the camera to the bottom of its neck strap near his waist, and turns to walk away. Seconds later, the three of us appear again in the Dorman film after stepping back up on the curb. I found a copy of the Dorman film on the internet as I was writing this book and was able to study it to some degree for the first time. The Internet copy is of poor quality, but the version restored in 2012 is much clearer. Our green camping stool is also visible in the Dorman film. It is sitting behind us as we are photographing. Until watching the restored film recently, I had never noticed the images in the Dorman film of Daddy, Mother, and me after we had stepped back onto the sidewalk and moved a few feet away in the direction of the triple underpass. Mother's white hair made her easy to pick out of the crowd. She is on my right. There is another woman with white hair (or perhaps she is wearing a light-colored headscarf) near me on my left. I do not know the identity of this woman. Not until viewing the restored version of the Dorman film was I able to identify my father at this point. He is standing right next to Mother and me. It appears that Daddy and others in a few of the frames look up suddenly as if they had just heard something. I believe Daddy was about to head down the hill to get another photo, but there was not enough time before the first gunshot sounded—only a second or two, if that, after I stopped filming. My first thought was that someone was throwing firecrackers out of a building window. I wasn't the only one who thought that. When I heard the first gunshot, there had been enough time for me to move back toward or onto the curb. I stopped and looked up at the buildings to see where the sounds were coming from. I didn't see anything, but I didn't know what I was looking for. I heard three gunshots, and sometime between the first and last, an unknown man grabbed my arm and pulled me to the ground. He held onto my arm until he thought it was safe to get up. I wish I knew his identity.

Some people might wonder if my belief that I heard three gunshots formed from hearing my father or others say they heard three gunshots, but that is not the case. I heard what I heard, and I have said so from the very beginning. My thoughts are my own and no one else has influenced them.

Everything happened very fast. The aftermath was very confusing, but I was not afraid. I got up off the ground and connected with my parents. The three of us stood quietly together for a few seconds amid the sirens and chaos, as we looked down from the plaza toward the triple underpass. Daddy calmly stated that he knew exactly what had just happened—someone just tried to shoot the president with a high-powered rifle, which he recognized from his Army training. He remained extremely calm throughout the entire ordeal. We all three did.

Many people ran toward the grassy knoll and behind it where there were railroad tracks. Daddy took his camera and followed the crowd. I can still see and feel Mother standing next to me with her arms folded, gazing down the hill over the plaza wall, waiting for Daddy to return. I know she must have been wishing he hadn't gone, but she didn't say much, if anything. When he finally returned, he brought with him a grim report.

Daddy took three more photographs while he was away from Mother and me, making a total of four color photos. Towner #1, as it has come to be known by the JFK assassination researchers' community, shows the presidential limousine as it turned around us at the corner of Houston and Elm. His three subsequent photos include two views toward the grassy knoll/triple underpass area from Elm, and one photo taken on the grassy knoll. Towner #2, the first of his grassy knoll photos, shows the backs of two men in suits in the foreground and a police officer kneeling on the left of frame on the south side of Elm with his service weapon drawn and aimed toward the north. Towner #3, Daddy's third photograph, shows the same perspective as Towner #2, but with no cars and fewer people. Towner #4, his fourth and last photo, is of a man later identified to me as Charles Brehm, a close eyewitness to the president's fatal gunshot wound. Standing on the grassy knoll, Daddy took that photo showing a visibly shaken Mr. Brehm with a crowd of people around him listening intently to his gruesome eyewitness account that someone shot the president in the head. Daddy said he thought Mr. Brehm had probably been standing about fifty feet from the president's limousine when the bullet hit President Kennedy in the head. While Daddy was behind the grassy knoll on the railroad tracks, he saw a man dressed in white standing on a railroad car. He described the man as a porter and said someone in the crowd asked the man if he had seen anything. In an email to me dated September 26, 2012, Gary Mack, curator of The Sixth Floor Museum at Dealey Plaza, said that the man Daddy described as a porter was apparently Carl Desroe. It is a shame Daddy did not get a picture of this man. I am sure he regretted it. He probably regretted not taking as many photos as possible, although I never heard him say so.

I do not remember whether Daddy asked me before he went down the hill or after he returned, but he calmly asked me if I had used up all of the film in the movie camera. I told him I had not yet heard the film clicking inside the camera, so he told me to keep filming and to pan slowly up and down Elm until I heard the film run out inside the camera. After I finished using up the rest of my film, I took my place beside Mother, and we patiently waited together as we watched the nightmare unfold around us.

Eventually, we made it back to our car. The drive home was long and silent, except for the news broadcasting on the car radio. All the way home, we listened to unconfirmed reports that the president was dead. As soon as we walked in the house, we turned on the radio and listened while Mother made sandwiches for lunch. We soon heard the official report that President Kennedy was dead. All I could do was nibble on the sandwich set before me. Then my parents asked me if I wanted to return to school, which was the original plan. I had

Tina Towner

not considered *not* going back to school, so without giving it much thought, I decided to go back, and my parents let me. I probably shouldn't have.

Back at school, I became confused. I checked in with the attendance office and went to class. Of course, no classes were actually in session. Dumbfounded students and teachers sat at their desks listening to the horrible news over the loud speakers in the classrooms. My friends knew I had gone to see the presidential motorcade, but no one knew I had been at the actual assassination site. The questions began. When I told them where I had been standing, looks of disbelief showed on their faces. It was hard for it to register with anyone that I was actually at the assassination site and was a witness. More importantly, it had not registered with me either—until I began talking about it with the other students and noticed their reactions. My classmates didn't dwell on it with me, and the teacher just looked at me helplessly. Someone asked me why I had returned to school. I had no idea. Neither the kids nor the teachers knew what to say to me. I was totally lost and numb, but I made it through the rest of the day somehow.

As is widely known, alleged assassin, Lee Harvey Oswald, fled to Oak Cliff where Officer J. D. Tippit ultimately spotted him. Oswald shot and killed Officer Tippit, and the police later apprehended him at the Texas Theatre in Oak Cliff, a place I frequented which was only three miles from my home. Officer Tippit's son Allen and I attended the same high school, but I did not know him. I am not sure if we attended the same junior high school in 1963. This sequence of violent events disturbed many students, but in 1963, schools offered no such thing as grief counseling. We dealt with it on our own the best way we could.

My parents and I were dazed and didn't know what to say or do with ourselves the rest of the weekend. We spent the days immediately following the assassination keeping up with the news reports and fielding questions from family and friends. Continuous coverage of the assassination and subsequent events dominated the airwaves. We had a big black and white television console in our den, and I had a black and white portable television in my room, which I stayed glued to all day on the day of the funeral. The indelible images of President Kennedy's funeral procession completely mesmerized me: Mrs. Kennedy in her black veil holding the hands of her two very young children, three-year-old John-John saluting his father, the riderless horse, and the endless solemn drum cadence. I soaked it all in. I still did not recognize the global or even national significance of what I had witnessed.

On the day of the assassination, the local television and radio news broadcasts immediately began directing anyone who had taken any pictures at the assassination site to turn the negatives over to (I believe) *The Dallas Morning News*. Maybe *The Dallas Morning News* was not the only one asking this, but that is where Daddy dutifully hand delivered his undeveloped film. He submitted the undeveloped roll of film from his Yashica and the undeveloped reel of film from the movie camera, as requested, assumedly, by the authorities. I did not go with him. He said he received a receipt for them, but I never saw it. Hindsight told Daddy and me that readily turning our pictures over to *anyone* was not a wise decision, but this type of recorded event was unprecedented, and no one (not even the authorities) seemed to know how to handle it. A short time later, Daddy began to worry that he might never see our film and negatives again, but we did. He said the authorities had possession of our film for several weeks. I cannot verify that, but I suspect he waited much longer than he should have waited for the materials to be returned to him, and it felt like it was much longer than several weeks. In 1996 during an oral history by The Sixth Floor Museum, Daddy said *The Dallas Morning News* told him when he inquired about the status of his pictures that the FBI had taken the film from them to study.

For the digital generation of readers, remember that in 1963 photos and movie film had to be developed before they could be viewed. At the time Daddy submitted the negatives to *The Dallas Morning News,* we had no way of knowing exactly what we had captured on film. We generally knew where we had been standing but not exactly. We were not sure what was in the background of Daddy's photo of the presidential limousine. We did know that the Texas School Book Depository Building had to be in the background of my film, but we were unsure how many floors of the building I had captured, which we learned when we watched my film for the first time. We were very anxious to get our images returned to us.

The Thanksgiving and Christmas holidays followed on the heels of the president's assassination. The undercurrent of each holiday was a solemn one, but Mother and Daddy tried to make them as normal and happy as possible. Thanksgiving meant a big turkey dinner—maybe a ham, too—with all the fixings, including cornbread dressing, sweet potato casserole, mashed potatoes with giblet gravy, green beans, fruit salad, tossed salad, and rolls or homemade bread, followed by cakes, pies and cookies. Each Thanksgiving Day also included a hike through the woods, which served the purpose of getting everyone out of Mother's way while she either prepared the meal or cleaned it up. We tried to put the assassination away for a while.

*First, middle, and last frames
from motorcade segment of my film,
showing the presidential limousine
as it turns around us at the corner of Houston and Elm.
Photographed by Tina Towner.
November 22, 1963*

© *1983 Mary C. Barnes (Tina Barnes)
All rights reserved.*

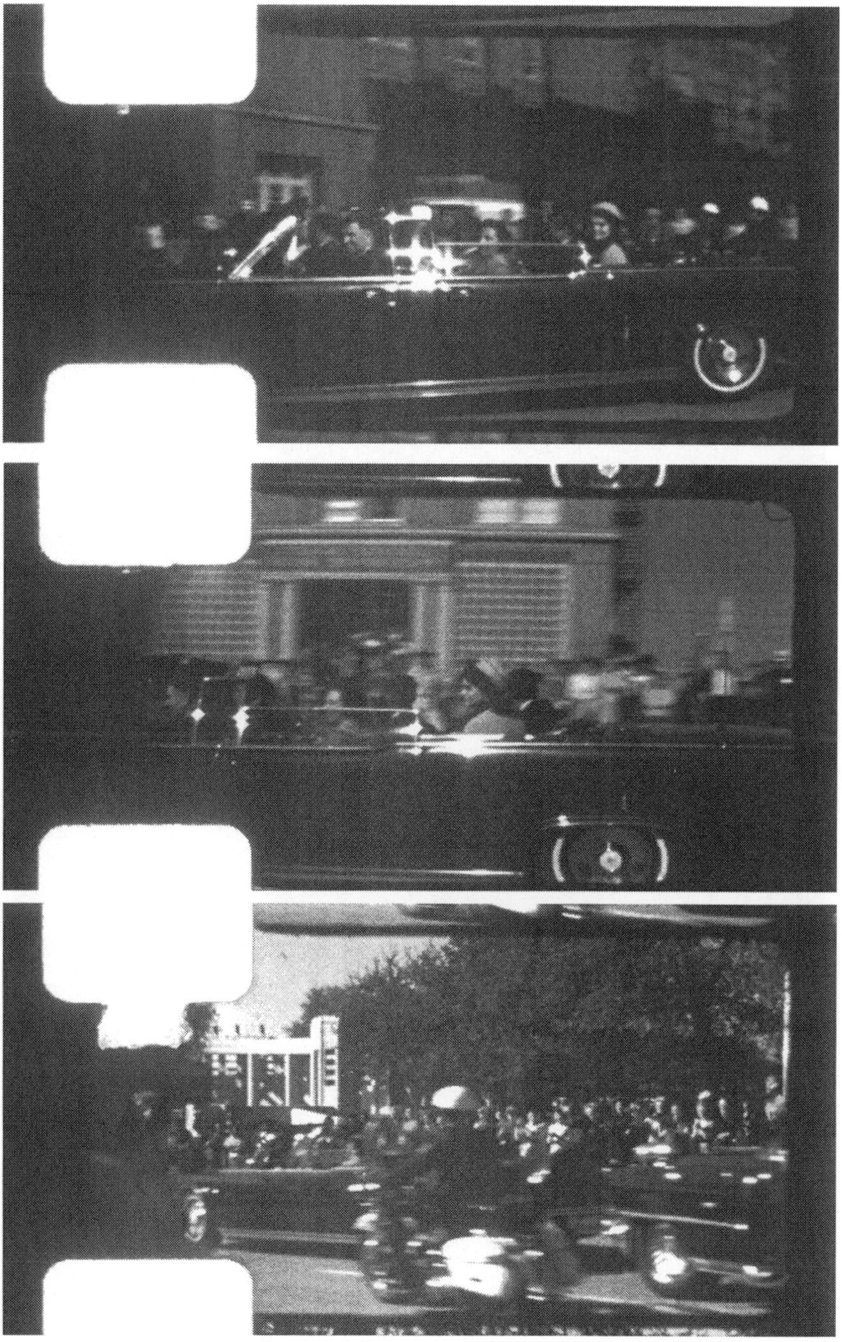

First, middle, and last frames from grassy knoll segment of my film, showing Elm Street and grassy knoll area, taken to use up end of reel. Photographed by Tina Towner. November 22, 1963

© *1983 Mary C. Barnes (Tina Barnes)*
All rights reserved.

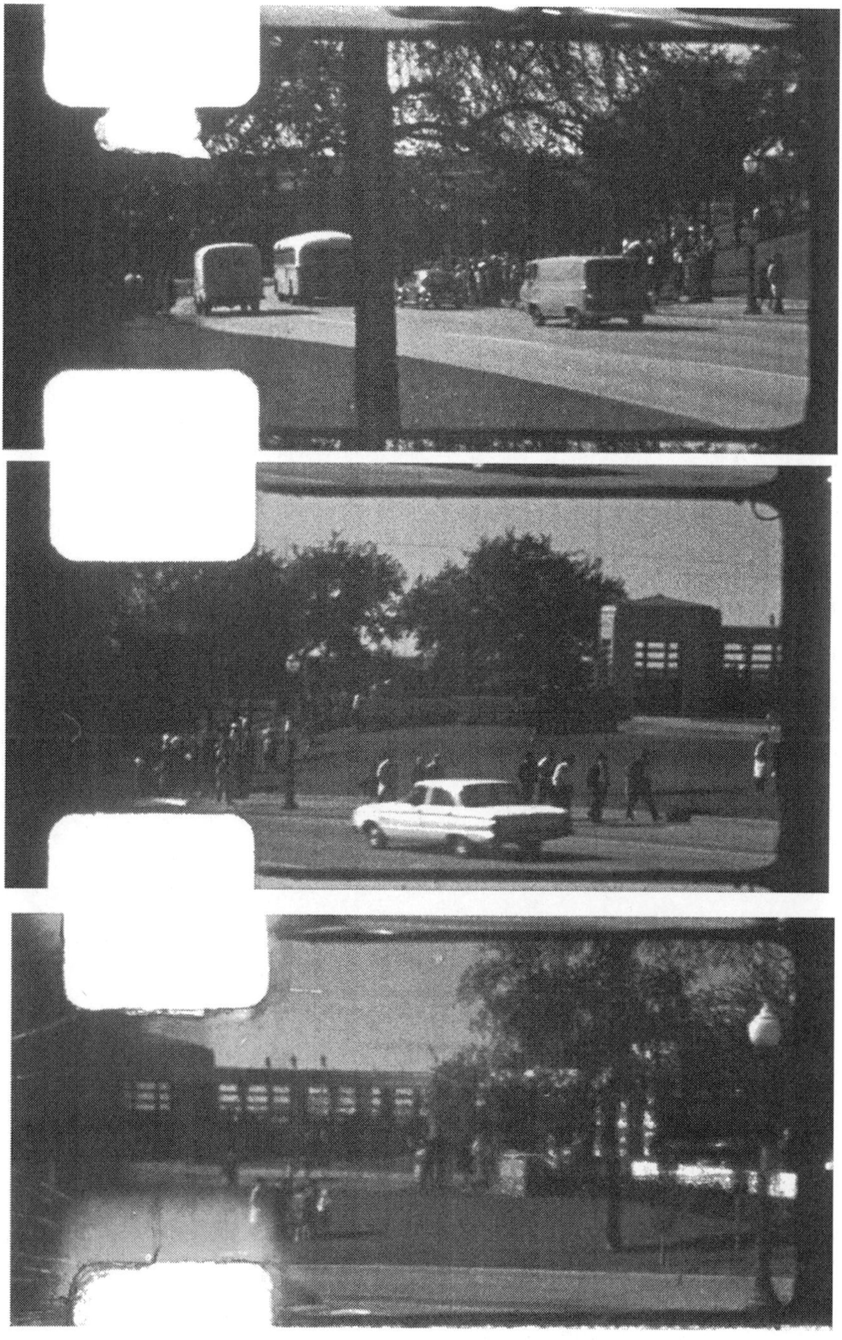

Towner #1
*Presidential limousine as it turns around us
at the corner of Houston and Elm.
Photographed by James M. Towner.
November 22, 1963*

*© 1967 1996 Mary C. Barnes (Tina Barnes)
All rights reserved.*

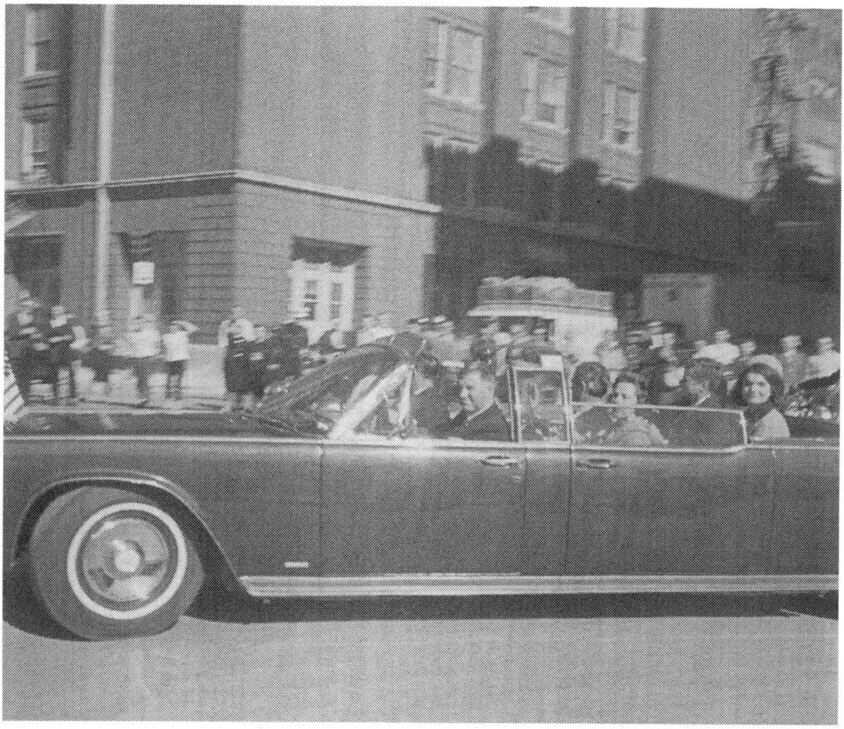

Towner #2

*Looking down Elm toward the triple underpass.
Photographed by James M. Towner.
November 22, 1963*

*© 1967 1996 Mary C. Barnes (Tina Barnes)
All rights reserved.*

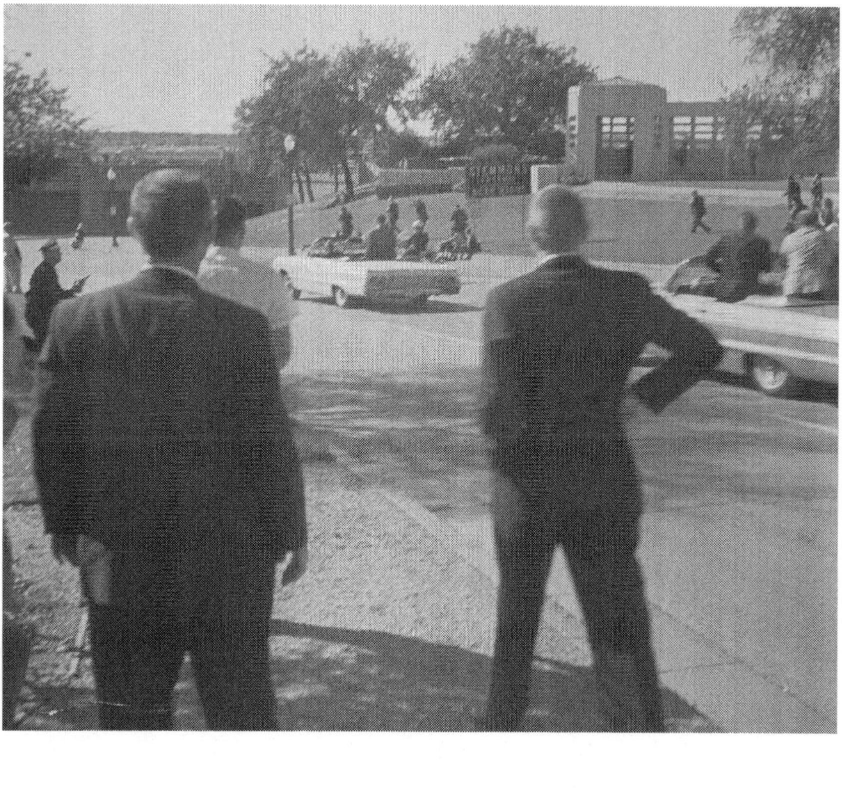

Towner #3

*Looking down Elm toward the triple underpass.
Photographed by James M. Towner.
November 22, 1963*

© *1996 Mary C. Barnes (Tina Barnes)
All rights reserved.*

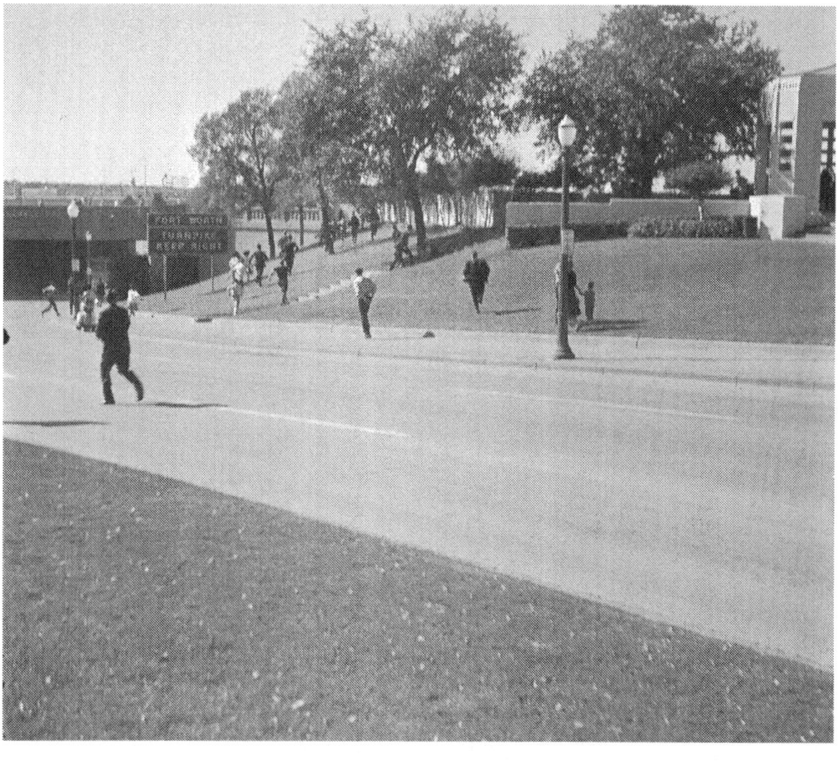
FORT WORTH
TURNPIKE
KEEP RIGHT

Towner #4 ~~Howard~~ Charles

Eyewitness ~~Howard~~ Brehm
standing on grassy knoll.
Photographed by James M. Towner.
November 22, 1963

© *1996 Mary C. Barnes (Tina Barnes)*
All rights reserved.

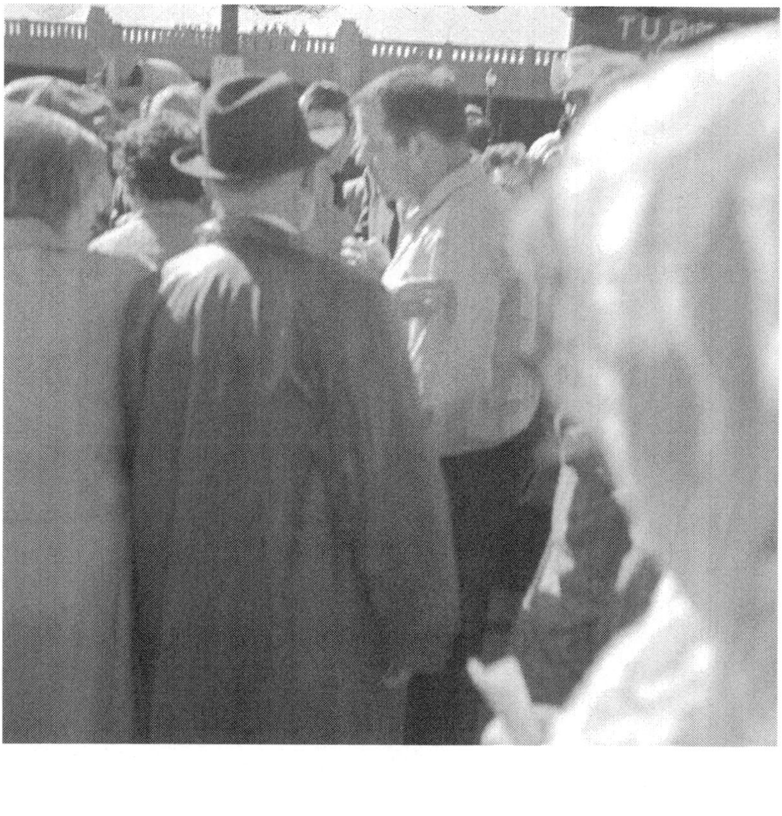

*The Towners on the corner of
Houston and Elm Streets,
photographing the presidential limousine,
taken from 4th floor window of TSBD.
Photographed by Elsie Dorman.
November 22, 1963*

*© 1967 The Sixth Floor Museum at Dealey Plaza
All rights reserved*

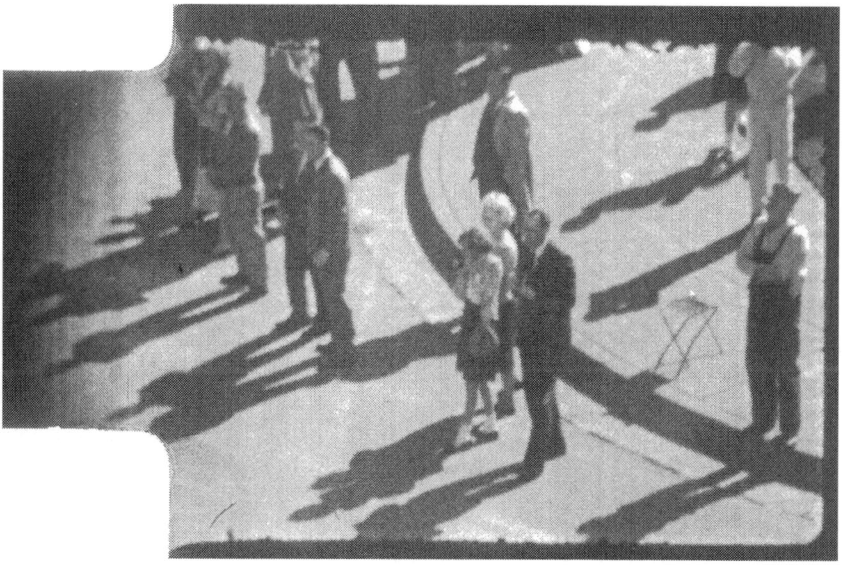

*Yashica 44 twin lens camera
used by James M. Towner on
November 22, 1963.
Dean Bentley, Photographer.*

Courtesy The Sixth Floor Museum at Dealey Plaza.

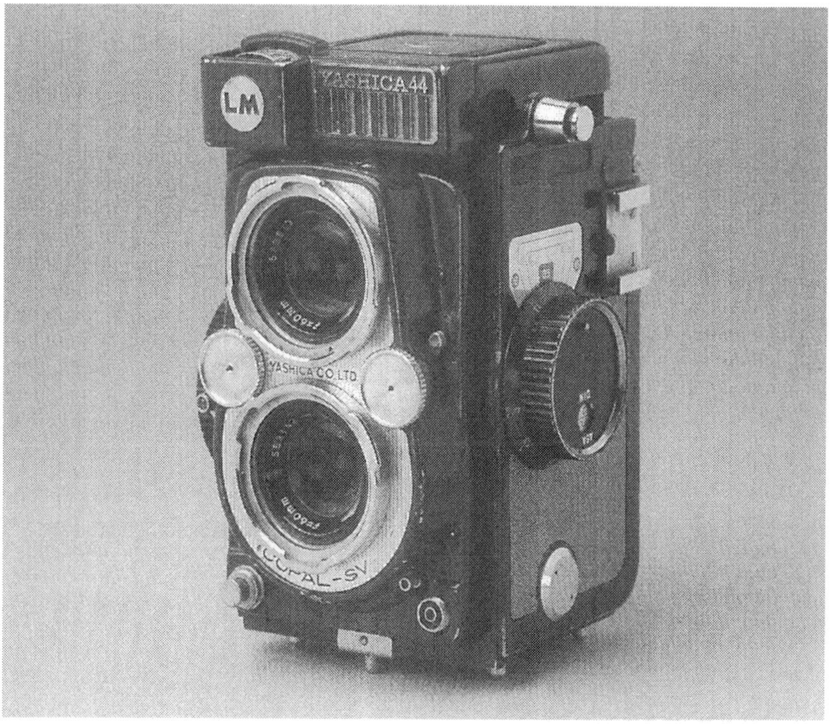
LM
YASHICA 44
YASHICA CO. LTD.

*Sears Tower Varizoom 8 mm camera
used by me on
November 22, 1963.
Dean Bentley, Photographer.*

Courtesy The Sixth Floor Museum at Dealey Plaza.

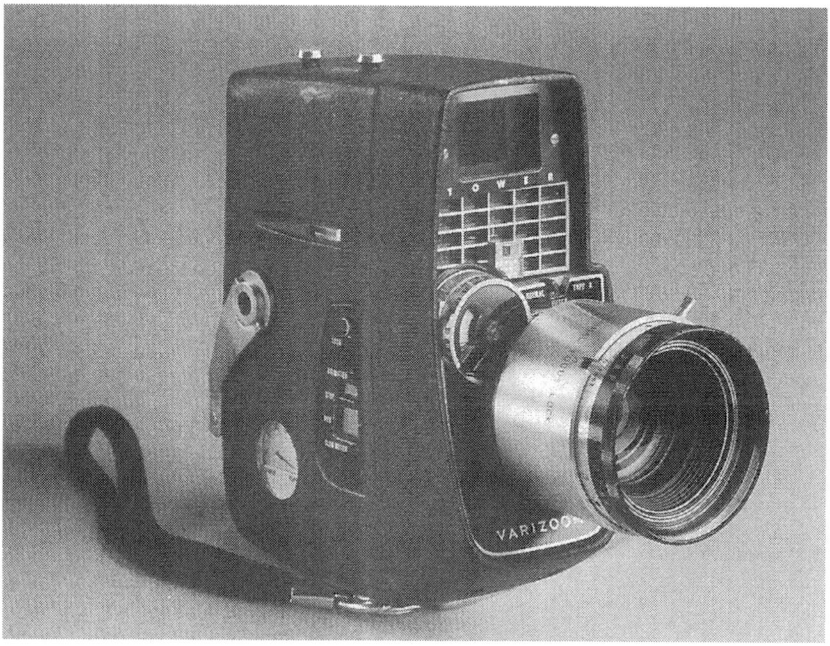
TOWER

Me at home.
Photographed by James M. Towner.
1963

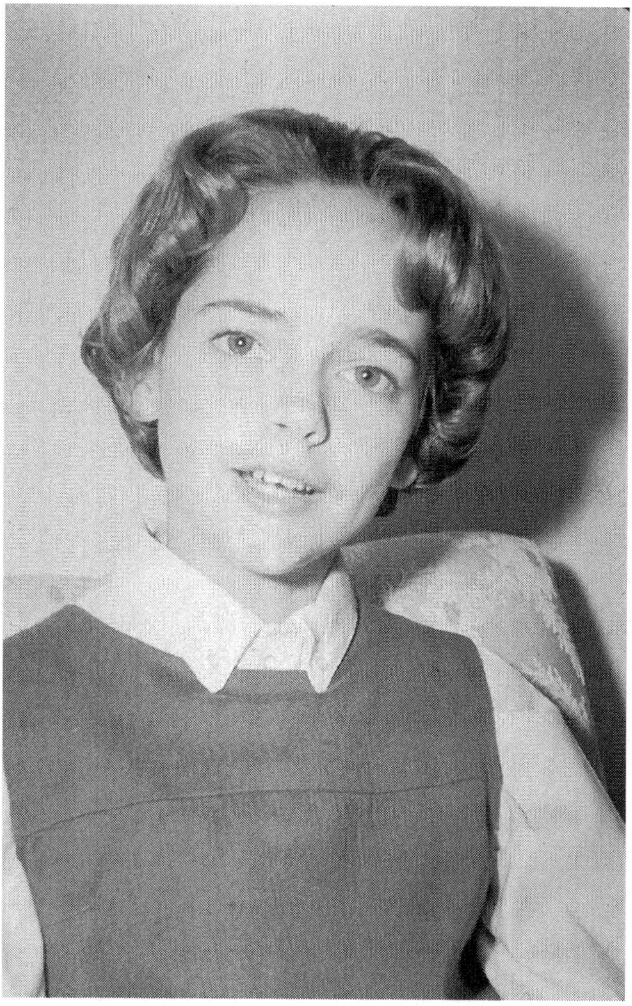

*Me and Sears Tower Varizoom
and Yashica 44 twin lens cameras
at JFK camera exhibit.
Gerald R. Ford Museum
Grand Rapids, MI
Photographed by Tony Goebel.
October 2, 1999*

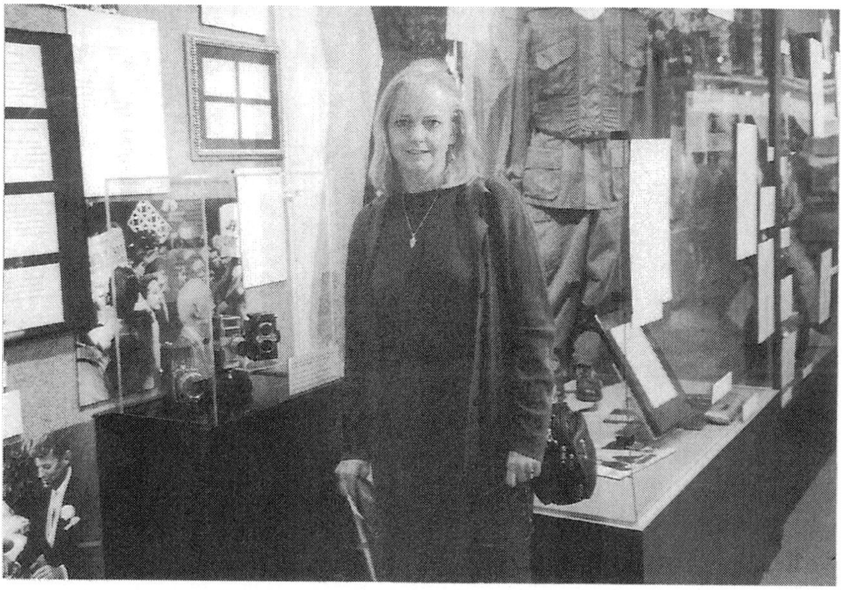

*Receipt for film from
Select Committee on Assassinations.
U.S. House of Representatives
12/29/77*

Select Committee on Assassinations
U.S. House of Representatives
WASHINGTON, D.C. 20515

12/29/77

Rec'd this date from Tina (Tocwer) Barnes the following items.
(4) slides - yellow container
(1) reel 8mm film - taped.

William Brown
Staff Investigators

To be returned as soon as possible (WB)

CHAPTER 3

The Rest of the '60s

The authorities returned to us (by mail, I think) the processed slides and film, but there is no record of when. I don't know if the slides and film arrived in the same package, but I think they did. We were anxious to see the images, and I helped quickly load the slides into the slide projector and the reel of film onto the movie projector. The beginning of the movie reel includes my sister Patsy and her husband Bob with their three-year-old son Mike, my sister Nancy going off to college, Daddy swimming with me in a motel swimming pool in Lubbock, and a segment of me in my T. W. Browne pep squad uniform as I leave for a junior high football game. The reel consists mostly of these home movies.

I sat with Mother and Daddy in the darkened room, and we watched. We had to sit through all of the home movies first, while we anxiously awaited the main event. The dreamy family home movies ended, and we

Tina Towner

braced ourselves for the nightmare to follow, but the film at the end of the reel began slapping the projector as the spool ran out before we got to the assassination. We all gasped, literally. There was no JFK film—or so we thought. Our hearts sank momentarily; but when I removed the reel from the projector, I discovered there *was* more film on the reel. Someone had separated the JFK portion of the film from the rest of the reel. Showing extreme patience with the situation, Daddy spliced it back onto the reel, and we sat, eyes glued to the movie screen, watching the final few seconds of John F. Kennedy's life as he waved to the crowd. We were finally able to see what images we had captured.

Only the first floor of the TSBD building is visible in the background of my film, and it is a blur due to my panning the camera. None of Daddy's stills showed any part of the TSBD building. We watched my film again and again. Doing so involved running the film to the end until it ran out of the projector feed, rewinding the entire reel, reloading, feeding it back into the projector, and starting it all over again. The projector did have a reverse feature, and we used it a couple of times, but Daddy did not want to damage the film, so he quit. The projector also had a pause mechanism, but pausing the film risked burning it. The approximate length of the motorcade portion of my film is about fifteen seconds. The total footage is about twenty-four seconds in length, including the motorcade portion and my pan of Elm from the grassy knoll to the Texas School Book Depository Building, using up the remainder of the spool. The *exact* length in seconds is undetermined, because the actual speed of the camera is still unknown. Gary Mack, curator at The Sixth Floor Museum at Dealey Plaza, told me someone would need to test the camera in order to determine the speed at which it recorded. To my knowledge, this has not been done.

Our family didn't talk much about the assassination. I did not know what to say when someone asked me about it. One night, maybe a year or two after the assassination, I was in my bedroom listening to a local late night AM radio talk show. The subject was the assassination. Conspiracy theories were already running rampant, and the talk-radio host had some caller on the phone with a crazy theory. For some reason, after listening to that caller, I felt the urge to call in to the program myself. When the host answered my call, the only words I managed to get out before he jumped all over me were that I was open-minded about the assassination. Brilliant. He responded with something that challenged me and my "open-mindedness." I felt like he was making fun of me, and I promptly and abruptly hung up without saying another word. I obviously had not thought through the process of making this phone call, and I had no idea at the time what I wanted to say to him or why. He scared me so much I have never called into a radio program since. I have no idea what his name was. (Maybe this is why I don't like to be interviewed.)

Years went by before anyone contacted my parents or me about the assassination. I wonder why the media did not contact us, and I have never heard anyone try to explain why the police, FBI, or other authorities did not. They most certainly knew about us, if only because Daddy submitted our film to the newspaper. I believe this shocked Daddy.

The first time anyone contacted us was four years after the assassination in 1967 when *Life* magazine called. I do not know if *Life*'s initial contact with Daddy was by telephone or by letter, but the first letter in my father's files from *Life* has a date of October 11, 1967. Its contents lead me to think there must have been some previous contact, because it goes right into the details of a proposed licensing agreement. On November 24, 1967, *Life* published a cover article entitled, "Why Kennedy Went to Texas," together with some of the unpublished images taken by me, my father, and eight other eyewitness photographers. In the front of this 1967 issue, on page three in the "Editor's Note," George P. Hunt, managing editor, stated that soon after the assassination, my father contacted Patsy Swank, a Dallas correspondent for *Life* magazine. Apparently, *Life* chose not to interview us at that time, but the editor's note went on to say that in the summer of 1967, *Life* discovered that Elsie Dorman had been taking movies of the motorcade from the fourth floor of the Texas School Book Depository building, where she worked. Accompanying the editor's note of that issue of *Life* was a thumbnail image of a frame from Ms. Dorman's film, clearly showing my father, my mother, and me while Daddy and I are in the process of photographing the president's limousine. Per the editor's note, after the representatives of *Life* viewed the Elsie Dorman images in the summer of 1967, they contacted Patsy Swank in Dallas to find out if she perhaps knew who we were. She identified us, subsequently contacted us, and she and her crew came to our home on Ovid Avenue in Oak Cliff to interview the three of us. Daddy did most of the talking during the interview and licensed our JFK images to *Life* for the November 24, 1967, issue of the magazine. I was seventeen years old, although the photograph they printed of me in that article made me look more like I was still thirteen. I was wearing braces on my teeth.

Our JFK images and other previously unpublished assassination pictures taken by other bystanders appear in the middle of an article written by Governor John Connally entitled, "Why Kennedy Went to Texas." The iconic photograph taken by John Dominis of Governor Connally holding his white hat appears on the cover of the issue. The Towner portion of the article is subtitled, "Close-ups by a father and his daughter" and reads as follows:

> "To get a good view, the family of Civil Engineer Jim Towner came an hour early to the motorcade route and stationed themselves at the corner of Houston and Elm, directly across from the Book Depository...Towner remembers noticing people in some of the Depository windows, one of whom he now believes was Oswald. As the presidential car slowly turned the corner just 25 feet in front of them, past the Dal-Tex building, Towner took the picture below. [See Towner #1 image] Meanwhile, Tina, the Towners' 13-year-old daughter, was using a movie camera to film the procession passing in front of the Book Depository... up to within moments of the first shot. She stopped when all she could see was the rear of the President's car. At the sound of shots she shouted, "Some dummy is lighting firecrackers!" But her father, an experienced rifleman, knew better. He sprinted down the motorcade route and took one final picture." [See Towner #4]

That issue of *Life* published "Towner #1" (Daddy's photo of the presidential limousine), along with "Towner #2" (view down Elm toward the triple underpass showing a police officer with his gun drawn), and three frames of poor quality from my motion picture film. The photograph *Life* took of my father, which they printed in that issue, was unflattering. He did not wear a coat and tie and regretted it immensely. Most of the other male subjects did wear coats and ties for their pictures, and the difference was dramatic. Daddy hated that photograph and commented that he looked like a thug.

A letter to Daddy from *Life* dated November 17, 1967, indicates he sold them a six-month option to license the film for a price to be negotiated later. Another letter of agreement from them dated December 6, 1967, indicates he gave them permission to use his stills in a proposed motion picture project and to keep the original stills for a period of six months for that purpose. I am not sure if *Life*'s motion picture project ever came to fruition. I found no further agreements in the files relating to that project, so I assume it did not. After *Life* published the November 1967 issue, authorities still had no interest in talking with us.

I found an interesting letter in Daddy's files dated December 10, 1967, from David Lifton, author of *Best Evidence* published in 1981. The letter followed up on a phone conversation Mr. Lifton had with my father a few weeks earlier concerning Lifton's licensing copies of Daddy's stills. According to my files, Mr. Lifton was still a graduate student at Cornell University at the time. There was no other documentation following up on this letter.

Around the first of the year in 1968, my father received a letter from Vincent Guarino, senior editor of *'Teen* magazine, asking if I would be interested in writing a two thousand word account of my experience on November 22, 1963, for the magazine. Mr. Guarino saw the 1967 *Life* magazine article and was interested in my teenage perspective of what I saw and felt on November 22, 1963. I said yes, and my article entitled, "View From the Corner," appeared in the June 1968 issue of *'Teen*. I was eighteen. After I submitted the article to *'Teen*, Mr. Guarino wrote a letter to my mother complimenting my writing skills and saying my story was just what he had hoped it would be. He also said any editorial changes to the story would be minimal due to how well I wrote it. It didn't appear to me that *'Teen* edited the published article at all. Mr.

Guarino sent photographer Joe Laird to my house, who photographed me holding my historical Sears Tower Varizoom camera. I wore a dress I made, and I was still wearing braces. The photo was almost a full page in size. (I contacted Hearst Publishing in 2011 and tried unsuccessfully to obtain permission to include the photo in my book.) Another photograph he took that day shows me "romping" with my dog Charlie. Mr. Guarino asked the principal of my high school, William P. Durrett, for permission to photograph me at school, but that request was denied. In a letter to me dated April 23, 1968, Don Aly, senior editor of *'Teen*, congratulated me for my "interesting slant on a news event that has been reported by just about everyone except a teenager." During the process of soliciting me to write this article, Mr. Guarino wrote some very nice letters to my parents. My files contain six letters from *'Teen*.

While writing this book, I opened two pieces of fan mail I received after the *'Teen* magazine story was published—both from the same person, a girl named Eileen in Pennsylvania. I had not opened these letters in decades. *'Teen* forwarded the first letter to me, and I knew I must have sent a reply to her first letter, because she sent me a second letter addressed to my home. While I was reading her first letter, I was wishing I had kept a copy of my reply. Then I opened the envelope with her second letter and found, to my joy, a hand-written draft I kept of my reply to her first letter. I couldn't believe it! Keeping that draft showed some foresight on my part.

In July 1968, as a result of and immediately following the June *'Teen* magazine article, the *Dallas Times Herald* awarded me the "Top Teen" award. I received a certificate and cover letter acknowledging my award, which Congressman Fred Orr of the Texas State House of Representatives signed.

Neither my parents nor I heard from any other media or authorities pertaining to the assassination until the US House of Representatives Select Committee on Assassinations reopened the case in the 1970s.

I was a member of the Oak Cliff Presbyterian Church Westminster Youth Choir for three years in 1966, 1967, and 1968. Each summer the group of about seventy-five teens took a two-week singing tour to churches around the United States. We traveled in three Greyhound buses and stayed with church members. In 1967, the group visited Arlington Memorial National Cemetery, where I visited the Kennedy gravesite for the first time. I was seventeen. It gave me a very strange feeling to be there and to realize I was also at Dealey Plaza during the assassination only a few years earlier. Oddly, it felt like it had been a very long time since the assassination. I guess that was because the lapse of time between 1963 and my trip to Arlington Cemetery in 1967 was nearly twenty-five percent of my life. While the choir was en route to California in 1968, Sirhan Sirhan assassinated Robert F. Kennedy at the Ambassador Hotel in Los Angeles. When I returned home several friends facetiously asked me if I happened to photograph that assassination, too.

I married my college sweetheart in 1969 and changed my last name to Barnes. My last name remained Barnes until early 2003 when I married Eugene Pender. My three children are Barnes.

CHAPTER 4

1970-1979
The Postal Connection

Daddy had a difficult time talking about the assassination for the rest of his life. He, Mother, and I answered questions if asked, but not many people did, other than infrequent questions from family members and close friends. In 1972, when my parents moved away from Dallas to Hamilton, Texas, Daddy asked me to take over the custody and management of our pictures. As I think back on this, his decision must have been a huge one for him. I was married with a child, but I was only twenty-two years old. I never questioned him about why, because I thought I knew why—they were moving away and didn't have a secure way to store the images. He handed over to me his original Kennedy slides and my original movie film, asking only that, for as long as he lived, I maintain control of the pictures and share equally with him any income produced by the pictures. He also suggested to me that I keep a written record of everything to do with our film and photos, including notes to the file, and I have tried to follow his advice.

At some point during the 1970s, I put our most valuable JFK materials into a safety-deposit box at a bank. I had some transparency copies and prints made of the slides, but we did not view the film often. Years at a time went by when we didn't view it at all. It was an ordeal to do so, because the movie projector and screen had to be set up. More importantly, we also did not want to disturb the film. With the advent of VCRs in the 1980s, under my supervision, I had the film and stills transferred to video tape, which made them easier to view.

Immediately following the Kennedy assassination, people interested in researching the assassination were usually referred to as Kennedy buffs. Neither my parents nor I were ever what anyone would call buffs. Soon, the term buff took on a disrespectful tone, and, in time, Kennedy buffs were more respectfully referred to as Kennedy enthusiasts or Kennedy researchers.

In the 1970s, I began receiving occasional inquiries from Kennedy assassination researchers. In the mid- to late 1970s, I was most often contacted by a man named Penn Jones who lived in the Dallas area. I also communicated with R. B. Cutler, who was in the process of writing *The Umbrella Man* at the time he first contacted me. Mr. Cutler used two of my father's photographs in his book *Seventy-Six Seconds in Dealey Plaza: Evidence of Conspiracy*. Pertaining to the "Towner #2" photo, he made the following statement in his book reflecting my father's attitude toward licensing our photos: "This print is from an early commercial copy of the original negative which Tina Barnes managed to pry from her father in '76 before they were persuaded by local researchers to go 'public.'"

In March 1977, I drove to Fort Worth, Texas, and met with a man named Jack White, a Kennedy researcher. I made the connection with Mr. White through our residential mail carrier. One day I had a phone call from our mail carrier, who recognized my name when he delivered a piece of mail addressed to Tina Towner Barnes. He was, of course, a

Kennedy enthusiast, and he knew Jack White in Fort Worth. These two individuals and a third person were interested in seeing my film, and since neither my dad nor I wished to let the film out of our sight, I told them they could look at the film, but only if I could stay with it at all times. Therefore, I went with them to Ft. Worth to a film-processing lab to study it. This is when and where I first discovered a mysterious splice in my original film. My parents and I had noticed a slight jump in the film in this spot, but we had never examined the film to check for splices. We just thought something had happened during the filming. The splice is where the limousine turns the corner at Houston and Elm. It appears to me that several frames are missing. The film jumps noticeably as the limousine turns onto Elm immediately before the Texas School Book Depository emerges into the background behind Jackie Kennedy's profile. The missing frames would be of her profile with the blue sky in the background or perhaps a frame or two as she crosses onto the TSBD background. This splice is not like one my father would have made. He taught me how to splice film using our home equipment, so I knew how to do it. This mysterious splice was more professionally made than the way Daddy would have been able to do it using the tools and equipment available to him at home. Daddy and I both knew the splice was not his handiwork. What I do know is the only times the film had been out of our hands prior to this discovery in 1977 was in 1963 when it was handed over to the newspaper in Dallas and again in 1967 when *Life* magazine had possession of it. The film did not leave our possession again until December 1977, when the House Select Committee took temporary possession of it. While writing this book and comparing the frames in the 1967 *Life* magazine with my film, I began to think that *Life* might have done it; however, looking at it more closely, I found that the frames they used appear to be still intact with my original film. The mysterious splice is earlier. I suppose it could have happened while in the hands of the newspaper or the authorities in 1963, but for what purpose I do not know. Maybe there was a problem while processing the negatives. Who did it and why are still mysteries. I have seen a few comments and conversations on the Internet surrounding this apparently controversial splice. I would love to know the story behind the missing frames, as would many other people, I am certain.

Another contact I made in the 1970s was J. Gary Shaw, who offered me some advice on copyrighting Daddy's stills, which I did in 1977. This process of copyrighting took a while. On July 22, 1977, I submitted to the US Copyright Office the required forms to register the four stills in Daddy's name, along with the two copies of the required set of four slides. On September 6, 1977, I received a disturbing notice from the Copyright Office saying they had received my application but the slides were not enclosed. I did not forget to enclose the slides. I enclosed them in a small box, which created some obvious bulk to the mailing envelope. On September 12, 1977, I resubmitted two more sets of slides to the Copyright Office, accompanied by a cover letter saying I was certain I had enclosed the slides with the original application. The Copyright Office finally registered the four, color stills. Copyright for the motion picture film did not take place until later.

I reiterate that for fourteen years after the assassination, authorities did not question my father, my mother, or me (obvious ear- and eyewitnesses). In 1977 that changed when a staff investigator for the US House of Representatives Select Committee on Assassinations contacted me. I was working in the corporate office of The Southland Corporation (7-Eleven) in Dallas at the time. On December 7, 1977, William Brown interviewed me over the phone regarding my possession of photographs/film. He asked what I had seen and heard, and I recall that his interest seemed obligatory, at best. The questions were few and brief, as were my answers. Maybe that was because I didn't have anything new or controversial to say. On December 29, 1977, William Brown and Martin J. Daly, another staff investigator, met me at my office at The Southland Corporation, where they briefly interviewed me again. At this meeting, I turned over to them my original movie film and transparencies for the temporary use by the Select Committee on Assassinations. I kept the original handwritten receipt for the pictures/film in my files, along with copies of other documents pertaining to this meeting. Staff Investigator William Brown's handwritten "Outside Contact Report" summarizes the materials I turned over to him as follows: "a- yellow oblong plastic container, containing (4) slides. b- vanilla colored square box, containing (1) reel of 8 mm film."

Gene Pender, the corporate controller of The Southland Corporation at the time, who was my boss and is now my husband, remembers that I seemed nervous about the meeting. I am not sure if my nerves were from the visit by the men in black or from telling Gene that two staff investigators with the House Select Committee on Assassinations were coming by the office to talk to me. This was the first time I had mentioned it to Gene, and I always became nervous when I brought the subject up to someone unaware of my experience in 1963. I began to tremble, as I showed him the 1967 *Life* magazine.

I last wrote a letter to the Select Committee inquiring about the return of my film and photos on November 29, 1978. A representative of the Select Committee scribbled a note on the back of an "Outside Contact Report" indicating my materials were returned to me on March 14, 1979. During the investigation by the Select Committee on Assassinations, no one asked to speak with my father and mother, who were in their mid-sixties at the time.

CHAPTER 5

1980-1989
The Sixth Floor Exhibit

There is one person I probably would have initially classified as a Kennedy researcher who turned that interest into a notable career. Gary Mack, now the curator of The Sixth Floor Museum at Dealey Plaza, took his interest in and research of the assassination of John F. Kennedy to a higher level. He is now a highly regarded and respected authority on the subject.

On the night of February 26, 1980, I received my first phone call from Gary, who was at that time with Z-97 radio in the Dallas/Fort Worth area. He had been asked by a man working as an advisor to the House Select Committee to call me to apologize on the advisor's behalf for not yet sending me the three copies of my JFK film that he had promised. The Committee still had possession of my originals that I handed over to them in December 1977, and they gave this advisor access to my film. I had patiently been waiting for copies of my film that I needed to submit with my copyright registration. It was an interesting conversation with Gary that night. In the course of discussing the subject of copyrighting my film, he told me he had been involved in JFK assassination research since 1975. Gary and I have stayed in contact with each other over the years, and the handling of my JFK materials has been much easier with his and The Sixth Floor Museum's support.

In September 1980, producer Jessica Schuman contacted me about a TV show called "Speak Up America," representing a new genre of TV called reality TV. They were interested in my point of view of the JFK assassination. I wrote a letter informing her of what images I possessed and told her I would be interested in talking to them if they wanted to do so. I received an invitation to join members of the "Speak Up America" production group and some other witnesses to the assassination at the corner of Houston and Elm on Wednesday, September 17, 1980. Marjoe Gortner, the host of the program, would interview me on camera. I did not have the presence of mind to bring my camera to this event.

This was the first time a television producer had contacted me, and I was very excited but nervous about being included in this program. Hoping to get into the spirit of the day, I decided to park in the same area where my parents and I parked on November 22, 1963, which had since become the parking area for facilities around the Hyatt Regency Hotel. I walked the same route my parents and I walked from Union Station to Houston and Elm, which helped me relax a bit. I had passed by Dealey Plaza a few times, but until this day, I had not actually visited Dealey Plaza since the assassination, which had been seventeen years.

As I walked down Houston toward the Texas School Book Depository, I could see the "Speak Up America" camera set up on the sixth floor in the window where Oswald allegedly perched. I arrived at 10:00 a.m., and eyewitnesses Mr. and Mrs. Phil Willis were waiting at the site. Around 10:15 a.m., Marjoe Gortner appeared, introduced himself to the Willises, and began his interview with them. I sat in the shade on the steps of the TSBD building and waited for instructions. When I saw the field producer, I walked across the street to introduce myself. Short interviews were recorded separately with the Willises and then with me, using the camera that was still aimed out of the sixth floor window. We each stood in the same place we stood on November 22, 1963.

When it was my turn, the camera was brought down to the street from the sixth floor window and additional close-up interviews were recorded with each of us still standing in our respective locations. Briefly recapped, Marjoe Gortner's questions included: what did you hear and see, where was your father standing, where were you standing, what did you do when you heard the shots, what did you think was happening, have your pictures ever been subpoenaed, have you or your father ever been subpoenaed, and did anyone ever question you? I learned a little about television interviews that day. I also discovered during this interview that in this type of setting it probably was not a good idea for me to use phrases, such as, Daddy's first shot, his second shot, I began shooting, etc. I am sure if the video from this production could be resurrected, it would be fairly entertaining, as I frequently tried to correct myself.

I talked to the field producer before I left, who said they would continue with some research the following week and would then decide if they wanted to use any of my pictures. They told me the show's planned airdate would be either September 26 or more likely October 3, 1980, possibly later. As I left, eyewitness photographer Jack Daniel began his interview. He photographed the presidential limousine as it came out from under the underpass. By the time I left, they still had three police officers to interview in the police station basement, and they were hoping to get an interview with Lee Harvey Oswald's widow Marina. They also had an appointment at the KFJZ studio to view some film Gary Mack had collected.

My "Speak Up America" day was memorable, and I eagerly anticipated the airing of the finished production in September or early October. The day it was scheduled to air on television, I tuned in to watch, only to find the entire show had been preempted at the very last minute because of something to do (I believe) with Muhammad Ali's Technical Knock Out by Larry Holmes. There was no "Speak Up America" that night. My big debut was a big letdown instead. However, a note I wrote to the files dated October 21, 1980, indicates the show did eventually air, and my interview was edited out (no surprise).

As I mentioned previously, because it was still difficult in the 1980s to get copies made of my 8 mm film, copyrighting the film did not happen at the same time as copyrighting the stills. I initially filed my application in 1978; however, because the House Select Committee still had my original film, I was still not able to get the necessary copies made of my own pictures. The Copyright Office postponed and eventually canceled my application, as per a notice from them dated July 6, 1979, saying I should resubmit my application when I had the required copies of the film to go with the application. I resubmitted the application in 1983.

At 6:30 p.m. on Saturday, July 16, 1988, my husband Rick Barnes and I were invited to join a group of people involved in the planning and design of The Sixth Floor Exhibit, which was the original name of The Sixth Floor Museum at Dealey Plaza. The exhibit would reside inside the former Texas School Book Depository building in Dallas. The original plan was to open the Exhibit sometime in November of the same year. The following information came from notes I made at the meeting that night. To the best of my knowledge, the information is accurate. The key participants were:

- Conover Hunt, curator of the Dallas County Historical Foundation who also served as the project director of The Sixth Floor Exhibit project
- Jackie McElhaney of the Historical Foundation
- Gary Mack, who was at that time an exhibit consultant for The Sixth Floor Exhibit and announcer with KXAS-TV in Fort Worth
- Charles A. (Chuck) Briggs and Abigail Porter of Staples & Charles, who owned a museum planning and design company in

1980-1989 The Sixth Floor Exhibit

Washington, DC. Mr. Briggs was formerly executive director of the Central Intelligence Agency and was with the CIA for thirty-four years before retiring and joining Staples & Charles, where he spent one year working on The Sixth Floor Exhibit project, as per The Sixth Floor Museum website.
- Allen and Cynthia Mondell, who wrote, produced, and directed the films seen in the permanent exhibit at The Sixth Floor Exhibit.
- Robert Groden, who served as a consultant for the Exhibit. Mr. Groden said he had been collecting photos pertaining to the assassination since he was eighteen years old. I remember he seemed almost giddy about meeting me.

We viewed several trays of interesting slides that Robert Groden brought with him that night—some of which the Exhibit probably used, but most probably not. It was such a treat for me to be able to listen to this creative group of people brainstorm about their vision of the Exhibit. I was virtually the fly on the wall that night. They were very interested in using Daddy's color photograph of the presidential limousine, which, I am proud to say, did end up enlarged and prominently displayed in black and white near the front of the Exhibit. I am not sure, but it is possible that the reflection visible on the side of the presidential limousine in my father's photograph is that of my parents and me. The meeting lasted until after 11:00 p.m. It was at this meeting that I saw, for the first time, a photograph taken of my parents and me from behind by Hugh Betzner as he tried to photograph the presidential limousine. I was still filming at the time. The photograph has more of us in the foreground than it does of the limousine. I love this photograph. I wanted to use it in my book, but I was unable to contact Mr. Betzner for permission. Seeing this photo at the meeting that night brought tears to my eyes. What an honor and a privilege it was for me to be included in this meeting!

The notes I took at the July 16, 1988, meeting were primarily so I could give my parents a written recap of the evening and hopefully make them feel somewhat included. They received an invitation to attend but declined because of their limited physical abilities. The

Sixth Floor Exhibit opened its doors to the public on Presidents' Day in 1989 and has continued to grow a highly respectable reputation and collection over the years.

There was a steady but subdued interest in my father's still photographs during the 1980s, but interest in my film has increased over time. I won't go into all of the numerous known copyright infringements of my film and photos over the years, except to say that any images photographed by me or my father for sale on the Internet are pirated. There have been a few infringements made by large companies who should have known better and who said they tried to contact me. I doubt this, however, because, even though I have changed addresses a number of times over the years, The Sixth Floor Museum at Dealey Plaza has always had my current address, anyone can reach me through them, and I have always tried to be responsive. In my opinion, since its inception the Museum has been the most logical place to begin looking for anyone having any connection to the assassination.

CHAPTER 6

1990-1999
The Photographers Gather

During the 1990s, there continued to be more interest in my film than in the still photographs my father took. I have granted licenses to use my film in a few productions: Oliver Stone's *JFK*; a number of local Dallas and national news programs; television news magazines; and a handful of documentaries on network and cable television, including The Discovery Channel, The History Channel, and National Geographic TV, all of which have been professional, trustworthy, and easy to deal with.

My oldest son Scott graduated in 1990 from Newman Smith High School in Carrollton, Texas, a suburb of Dallas. Since early elementary

Tina Towner

school, Scott dreamed of working in the movie industry, and he made his dream a reality. While still in high school and after his relentless persistence in trying to get hired by a company in the Dallas area named Victor Duncan, he finally succeeded and went to work part time for them. Victor Duncan furnished production equipment to movie and TV production companies. In 1990, while Scott was working for Victor Duncan, he surprised me at work with a telephone call from his work and rapidly began firing off questions to me about the assassination. Oliver Stone's *JFK* was in production at the time. Scott wasn't working on that movie, but it was the topic of conversation that day at his work. Eventually the topic turned to where each of his coworkers or coworkers' parents had been when they heard about the Kennedy shooting. When it was Scott's turn, he told them that his mother and grandparents were at the assassination site that day and that his grandfather and his mother took photographs and film. Unlike the usual silence that occurs in my presence, his coworkers immediately bombarded him with questions. It was at that moment he realized he didn't have all of the answers. Although the assassination has always been a facet of my children's lives, Scott (because he was the oldest) was the first to realize the historic significance of my witnessing the event. He and I spent about forty-five minutes talking about it on the phone that day. It was an interesting exercise for both of us, and I will always remember that phone call.

On Monday, November 22, 1993, I attended the dedication ceremony recognizing Dealey Plaza as a National Historic Landmark. The ceremony took place outside at Dealey Plaza at 11:30 a.m. This was an important event for Dallas, for the Dallas County Historical Society, and for The Sixth Floor Exhibit. Many people poured a lot of hard work into this project over the years, and I was thrilled to be included in this historic event.

My parents moved to Bonham, Texas, in early 1994, and later that year I moved to Bonham, which is about an hour and a half drive northeast from Dallas. On March 30, 1996, Gary Mack and Bob Porter from The Sixth Floor Museum came to Bonham to record our oral history for the Museum. Daddy's health was too frail to make the trip to Dallas, so Gary and Bob were kind enough to come to the house. The interview took several hours. My mother, father, and I sat around their heirloom oak table in the kitchen of their very small house. Also present in the room were their two dogs, Huck and HD (Hound Dog), which were both big noisy dogs. The dogs caused constant disruptions to the video recording, but we got through it. Gary and Bob exhibited extreme patience with their surroundings, which I really appreciated, but, having been so accustomed to the noisy dogs, I don't think I appreciated it as much as I should have at the time. Daddy seemed completely oblivious to how annoying the dogs were. Mother was not.

On Friday, November 22, 1996, The Sixth Floor Museum officially opened its camera exhibit, which included our two cameras and the cameras used by other eyewitness photographers at the Kennedy assassination. The event included a live interview of *Life* magazine's Richard Stolley by Jeff West, executive director at the time. I was happy that my father was able to attend, but Mother chose to stay home.

My parents and I were living in Bonham at the time. I picked Daddy up around 3:00 p.m., and we drove to downtown Dallas for the event. Along with me and my father, this gathering included other eyewitness photographers and/or family members. Prior to the six o'clock reception, at the suggestion of Patsy Paschall, an eyewitness photographer who was present at the event that night, the photographers gathered to share their stories with each other in the County Commissioners Court in the former Texas School Book Depository Building. Dr. Marian Ann Montgomery, the Museum's director of interpretation at the time, chaired this session of shared personal recollections. To my knowledge, this was the first and only time this many eyewitness photographers have been together. I learned from Gary Mack that evening that my father (age eighty-three) was the oldest living photographer at that night's event and I was the youngest. Each eyewitness photographer or surviving family member had an opportunity to address the group informally. I said only a few words before handing it over to Daddy to speak. He shared with the group that he was not afraid on November 22, 1963, that he recognized the shots as being from a rifle, and that he abruptly stopped what he was doing at the sound of the first gunshot, which came from right behind him, as he stood with his back to the book depository building. It is my opinion that the exact moment he recognized the gunfire is captured on Elsie Dorman's film. He tried to say more to the group but was overwhelmed and broke down in tears. It was a very emotional night for him and for all of us. The local Channel 8 news covered this event and interviewed several photographers, including Daddy, who was on the news that night! It was a good interview, and he handled himself very well. This was Daddy's only visit to The Sixth Floor Museum.

In 1996, at the suggestion of The Sixth Floor Museum and Gary Mack, my father and I changed the copyright registration for Daddy's four stills from his name to my name. This change was made to avoid any copyright-related problems if, for any reason, my father was unable to authorize licensing of the photos.

On Saturday, November 21, 1998, I attended an event at The Sixth Floor Museum at Dealey Plaza commemorating the thirty-fifth anniversary of the assassination. Gary Mack and Richard Ray organized and planned this impressive event, which included a panel discussion with Wes Wise, Bill Mercer, Eddie Barker, and Bob Huffaker. All, including Richard Ray, were local TV newsmen for KRLD-TV, now KDFW. Jeff West, executive director of the Museum at the time, moderated.

In 1999, I was contacted by the Gerald R. Ford Museum in Grand Rapids, Michigan, regarding their planned temporary exhibit called "The American Century" that would be open from April 10 through October 17 that year. They requested permission to include my father's and my cameras in this exhibit. The Sixth Floor Museum assisted with transferring the cameras, and I was able to travel to Grand Rapids to see the exhibit on October 2 with my friend, Tony Goebel. The exhibit included the two Towner cameras, along with a duplicate of Orville Nix's camera. As per Gary Mack, curator of The Sixth Floor Museum at Dealey Plaza, the FBI gave Mr. Nix a duplicate of his camera after damaging the original. The display was in an area that also included documents exchanged between President Kennedy and Premier Khrushchev during the Cuban Missile Crisis, cards from the speech Kennedy was carrying to deliver later that evening in Austin, Texas, and a letter written by Mrs. Kennedy to Richard Nixon during her last day at the White House. Listed in the marketing materials, among the lenders to "The American Century" exhibit were the following: other presidential libraries and museums, the Supreme Court of the United States, Smithsonian, the National Archives, The Sixth Floor Museum at Dealey Plaza, and various historical societies around the United States. I was honored to be included among such esteemed lenders.

CHAPTER 7

2000-2009
A Whole Other Life

On November 21, 2000, The Sixth Floor Museum at Dealey Plaza hosted another panel discussion, which was to include me and three other eyewitnesses: Orville Nix, Jr., Mal Couch, and Patsy Paschall; however, Ms. Paschall was not able to appear. Jeff West, executive director at that time, moderated in front of the *by invitation only* audience of about two hundred fifty. The father of Orville Nix, Jr., photographed the assassination from south of the motorcade, and Malcom Couch was a reporter in the motorcade. The film and photographs that the panel participants had taken were projected onto a screen during the discussion. Mr. Couch said he had not seen his own film in thirty-seven years. My father received an invitation to participate in this panel, but he and I discussed it and again agreed it would be too mentally and physically taxing for him to do so; therefore, he declined the invitation.

This was a very special night for me, because my son Chris and daughter Carley (ages 18 and 16, respectively) accompanied me to the event, and it was the first time the three of us had been to the Museum together. It was the first time Carley had ever been. My son Scott and his family were unable to attend. The evening also included dinner at The Palm in the West End. The three of us walked through the Museum after we arrived, and I showed Chris and Carley my father's photo display. Then we proceeded to the seventh floor where the program would take place. As soon as we walked in, I was met by Sam Childers (with the Museum), who immediately ushered me over to a KRLD radio reporter for an interview. Immediately after that, someone asked me to autograph a paper guidebook from the Museum and a book authored by Richard Trask. Chris and Carley were soaking it in, and this was all new to me, too. I didn't feel like my interview with the KRLD reporter went very well, mostly because of the last question he asked, which was what would I like for people to take with them after seeing my photos and hearing my story. I was unprepared to answer that question, and when I told Carley and Chris about it, Carley promptly replied that I should have said I would like people to feel a little of what it must have been like to witness this historic event. I gratefully tucked that bit of advice away for future use and included it in the introduction of this book. (Thank you, Carley.)

I spent most of the first hour that evening signing autographs and talking with interested guests. Early in the evening, while Chris and Carley looked on, the sound technician wired me for the panel discussion. He secured the battery pack to the back of my dress, attached the microphone to the front of my jacket, warned me that he would be testing the microphone and would be able to hear what I was saying, and Carley, Chris, and I most certainly gave him some laughs. Before the panel discussion began, I reminded Chris and Carley to turn their cell phones off and told them I would not look at them during the program, because I was sure doing so would make me laugh. They teased me later

2000-2009 A Whole Other Life

because someone else's cell phone did ring during the program, and I involuntarily looked right at them. They both had huge grins on their faces, and I quickly looked away.

I enjoyed being on this panel and, surprisingly, did not get butterflies. I was the only one of the three panelists who did not tear up. After the program, I signed more autographs and posed for a few more photographs. As the evening neared its end, I approached Chris and Carley, and Chris grinned and quietly and proudly said, "Our mom has another life—a whole other life." This event on November 21 was an eye-opener for them, and I was very proud to have them with me that evening. After the program, Chris, Carley, and I joined museum staff and other participants and their families for dinner. It was an enjoyable and memorable evening.

Chris and Carley grew up with the knowledge of my history with the Kennedy assassination. They knew Gary Mack and knew I was part of the program that night in 2000, but they did not expect the attention I received. I admit, I didn't either. I am uncomfortable in front of a camera or an audience, and my performance could not have been very impressive; but it was a far cry from the single-working-mom routine the kids and I were all too familiar with. Chris and Carley appeared to enjoy the evening and did not miss any subsequent opportunities to tease me about that night, as each of them (posing as me) simultaneously struck exaggerated faux celebrity poses for their imaginary paparazzi.

On November 26, 2000, I received an e-mail from Gary Mack with a copy of an Associated Press article dated November 24, 2000, written by Mike Crissey and published by *The Washington Post*. My name was mentioned in the article, which was about the acquisition of the Orville Nix Film by The Sixth Floor Museum at Dealey Plaza. In addition, various news articles about the November 21 Sixth Floor event appeared in local newspapers around the United States and possibly around the world.

It was in 2002, around Thanksgiving, while going through my dad's files after he passed away, I found some letters dated 1969 from a man who had sent him some copies of letters regarding the

Tina Towner

assassination. One letter dated November 22, 1969 indicated the author would like to have returned to him the photocopies of some letters and a newspaper article he had sent Daddy. He sent these materials to my dad to support a request for Dad's photos and to help explain who he was. The supporting documentation included a photocopy of a letter this man had received from J. Edgar Hoover about the assassination. After making this discovery, I did some research on the Internet and found an e-mail address for the author. I wrote him, received a reply, and subsequently mailed him the documents, after 30-plus years. He appreciated my actions and said he had all but forgotten about them.

In the fall of 2002, The Discovery Channel interviewed me for a documentary that aired in February 2003. It was part of the *Unsolved Histories* series and focused on the photographs taken by me and other amateur photographers at the assassination. I had a great opportunity to talk with a few of the other photographers or their surviving family members. Part of my interview took place at Dealey Plaza and part of it was recorded in a studio. The documentary used some of my interview but not all. While setting me up in the studio for the interview and testing the sound equipment, the interviewer asked me a few basic questions, such as, what my name was. I was divorced but was still using the last name of Barnes at the time. I was planning to marry Gene Pender within a few months, and I knew I would soon be changing my last name to Pender. I said my name was, "Tina Towner Barnes," followed by a long pause and a heavy sigh. I then interrupted the interviewer and asked if it would be OK to leave off "the Barnes." He told me that I could, of course, but I knew that the whole exchange must have looked ridiculous, as a copy of the unedited interview clearly shows. This, too, has been a source of more than a few family jokes at my expense, as if I couldn't remember my own last name. I wonder if anyone connected with the production thought it was as funny as my family did.

My daughter Carley attended The Art Institute of Dallas and graduated with an associate degree in 2004. One of her subjects was videography, and as a project of her studies, she videotaped an interview

2000-2009 A Whole Other Life

she did with me about the Kennedy assassination. Other than the fact that she did the interview at her apartment, over all, it was similar to the interviews I have done with professional journalists, and I was just as nervous. She received a good grade on this project.

In 2003, The Andy Warhol Museum in Pittsburgh, Pennsylvania, in conjunction with The Sixth Floor Museum at Dealey Plaza, opened a temporary exhibit to coincide with the fortieth anniversary of the assassination of President Kennedy. I gave them permission to use my film as part of that exhibit, which ran from November 22, 2003 through March 21, 2004. I was unable to attend the exhibit.

Also, in November 2003, a documentary entitled *JFK: Breaking the News* aired on KERA, the North Texas public broadcasting television station. KERA and The Sixth Floor Museum at Dealey Plaza produced this documentary, which included my film and Daddy's photo of the presidential limousine.

In October 2007, my husband Gene and I took a road trip to Washington, DC, and visited Arlington Memorial National Cemetery while we were there. This was my second visit to Arlington Cemetery, and I was much more touched by the Kennedy gravesite this time than I was in 1967. It felt strange to be there again and stirred even heavier reflection as I looked down this time to see Jackie Kennedy by John F. Kennedy's side.

In November 2007, the Sixth Floor Museum at Dealey Plaza opened an exhibit entitled "Filming Kennedy: Home Movies from Dallas." This exhibit included my JFK assassination film, along with all of the other Towner home movies on that same reel. It also included amateur home movies taken at the JFK assassination site by other eyewitnesses in 1963, along with the personal home movies on their reels and a few other artifacts. I received an invitation to attend the opening, and I hate to describe an exhibit pertaining to the death of a president as fun, but I really enjoyed seeing all of the personal home movies.

On February 1, 2008, I accepted an invitation to help launch the Museum's 2008 public programs by participating in a Q&A with Gary Mack. Anyone with paid admission to the Museum that day could attend the Q&A, which took place on the seventh floor. I was nervous about being the only subject at this event, but host Gary Mack did a great job making me feel at ease. The turnout for my appearance was bigger than I expected. After the Q&A and lunch, Stephen Fagin recorded another short oral history of me for the Museum (this time without my parents' barking dogs) to complement the one my parents and I made in Bonham in 1996. They also asked my husband Gene to record one—another very interesting day.

CHAPTER 8

2010 Forward Gearing Up

In September 2010, it became apparent to me that things were gearing up for the fiftieth anniversary of the assassination in 2013. Within one week I received three requests. The first request was for the use of my film in an overseas production. The second request was from Robert Stone Productions for an interview and for the use of my images pertaining to a documentary being produced for the National Geographic Channel. The third request was for an interview with Dr. Larry Sabato, University of Virginia Professor of Politics and Director of the University of Virginia's Center for Politics.

On Saturday morning, September 25, my husband Gene and I drove from Leander, Texas, to Dallas for my interview with Dr. Sabato. We arrived at The Sixth Floor Museum at Dealey Plaza around 2:45 p.m. I wasn't sure what to expect but was pleasantly surprised to discover the meeting was casual and relaxed. Megan Bryant, director of Collections and Intellectual Property, greeted us and showed us to the meeting room in the Museum's new offices across Houston Street from the Museum. Also invited to be part of this interview were Pierce Allman, a WFAA reporter at the time of the JFK assassination, and Bill and Gayle Newman. Widely circulated photos of the Newmans taken at Dealey Plaza in 1963 show the Newman couple on the grassy knoll after they had thrown themselves over their two-year- and four-year-old sons to protect them from the gunshots. The Newmans witnessed firsthand the gunshot to Kennedy's head. Eddie Barker, another prominent local Dallas reporter, received an invitation to this interview but was unable to attend. Also present were my husband Gene; Nicola Longford, museum director; Megan Bryant, director of collections and intellectual property; and Dr. Sabato's assistant Joe Figueroa.

The primary purpose of the interview was to discuss why each of us was at the assassination site that day and what each of our lives has been like since. It is an understatement for me to say it was interesting to listen to these other witnesses talk about that day. After talking with Mr. Allman, he and I thought perhaps he was the person who pulled me to the ground after hearing the first gunshots. He said he thought he was standing nearby and remembered pulling someone down. After viewing a few frames from the restored Dorman film, however, he said he did not think he was standing close enough to me. The interview lasted about two hours. I am disappointed that I did not think to take any photographs, but the Museum and Dr. Sabato recorded it.

Another big event for me was in April 2011. I received a call from Iwonka Swenson, with National Geographic TV, who requested an interview with me for a television documentary she was co-producing with Robert Stone Productions. The documentary was based on a theory by author and journalist Max Holland. It included a restored version of my film, along with other historical films from that day which had been restored for this project. I left home to drive to Dallas around 9:00 a.m. on a Sunday and met Mr. Holland, Mr. Stone (an award winning documentary filmmaker), Ms. Swenson, and other National Geographic personnel at Dealey Plaza.

They graciously invited me to meet them for lunch at Sonny Bryan's Barbeque restaurant in the West End. They treated me like part of the family, and I enjoyed talking with them. I appreciated the time Mr. Holland, Mr. Stone, and Ms. Swenson took with me, especially since I knew how extremely busy everyone was. At lunch, not knowing details of the documentary's premise, I asked Mr. Holland why he had chosen me to be one of the three eyewitnesses in the documentary. He answered that it was because of my film. After a quick lunch, our group walked back to Dealey Plaza, where I waited for my turn to interview. While waiting, I observed the production crew at work, and I observed the other observers, as there were many onlookers trying to figure out what was going on. Most of the onlookers that day were tourists who came to visit The Sixth Floor Museum and the grassy knoll area, and for them to be able to watch a TV production in progress using a limo replica and look-alike actors must have been an exciting bonus.

National Geographic Television hired actors to play the parts of the Kennedys and the Connallys in costume, who rode in a limousine replica owned by Nick Ciacelli. They filmed each eyewitness standing where each of us stood in 1963, while the limousine drove by in the background.

Before beginning the interviews, Max Holland visited with me for about fifteen minutes to describe his theory and to explain what he and NatGeo TV were investigating in this documentary. His theory is that the first gunshot was fired as the limousine finished its turn onto Elm, and the first bullet hit a traffic light mast and ricocheted away. If it had not hit the traffic light mast, his theory is that it would have hit something or someone in the limo. If that were what happened, it would mean the first shot was fired just as I finished filming and before Zapruder began filming. It would also mean that the gunman would have aimed more directly down from the sixth floor window toward where my parents and I were standing. Max Holland believes that my film is a very important piece of evidence, second in importance only to Zapruder's film.

My twenty-minute, on-camera interview began around 2:30 p.m. When we were finished, I took some photographs of the limo replica, and the owner Nick Ciacelli asked if I wanted to sit inside the limo while he took my picture, which I did. Next, they filmed the limousine with occupants as it turned around the Houston/Elm corner and drove down Elm. I sat in a chair on the walkway next to the NatGeo TV camera operator, who was filming from Zapruder's perch. I took a cell-phone video of the motorcade reenactment, also from the same angle as Zapruder's film was taken. This was all very surreal.

In November 2011, Iwonka Swenson, co-producer of the NatGeo TV documentary, and Dan Sullivan, owner and CEO of Image Trends, Inc., invited me to attend the annual conference of the Association of Moving Image Archivists (AMIA) being held in Austin, Texas, later that month. I was thrilled to receive an invitation. Image Trends, Inc. is the company that restored my film and the other assassination films for the Max Holland/NatGeo TV documentary. Prior to the conference, Dan Sullivan invited me to visit his office in Austin for a tour of his facility, a general explanation of how they restored my film, and an opportunity to view the JFK films they had restored for the documentary. He told me that, of the films they restored for this project, my film was in the best condition, although still deteriorating. I attribute the relatively good condition of my film to the fact that it has not been handled much by anyone since 1963. Mr. Sullivan complimented my teenage camera skills, mainly referring to how still I held the camera as I panned around the corner.

It is difficult to convey how good I feel about having the opportunity to restore not only my film, but also the other films, before it is too late. I can now see four things in Elsie Dorman's restored film that I could not see before. The first thing is that it is more obvious that Daddy holds his Yashica camera up to his eye to look through the viewfinder hole (it is actually a hole) while he takes his photograph of the presidential limousine. Second, there is a man dressed in what looks like a train engineer's cap and overalls standing to Daddy's left while we are in position for photographing the motorcade as it turns the corner. Third, Daddy and "Railroad Man", as he has come to be called, clearly speak to each other. Fourth, I noticed in the restored film that Daddy, Mother and I are standing near each other after moving back up on the curb after we took our pictures.

In a breakout session at the Association of Motion Images Archivists conference in Austin on November 18, Iwonka Swenson (National

Geographic) and Dan Sullivan (Image Trends, Inc.) used my film in a presentation about the restoration of my and other JFK films. At the beginning of the presentation, Mr. Sullivan announced to the audience that all of the JFK films they restored were very jumpy—except one—made by a thirteen-year-old girl named Tina Towner. He went on to describe my panning of the presidential limousine, as it turned the corner around my parents and me, as "perfect." He then announced that I was in the audience, and I actually heard a couple of gasps behind me. It is difficult to describe how I felt as I listened to the audience of approximately one hundred motion picture archivists applaud during my introduction. I was overwhelmed and surprised. Mr. Sullivan mentioned to me before the presentation that the attendees of the breakout session where my film would be presented would be very excited when they learned I was present in the room. He explained that these people were accustomed to working tediously in dark rooms with old films, never having an opportunity to meet the photographers, who had long since passed away. My afterthought was that having a "live" one in attendance did cause a stir.

The National Geographic TV documentary, *JFK: The Lost Bullet*, aired on November 20, 2011. I was apprehensive about seeing it. I wasn't a pro at this, and I didn't always end up in the final cut; but Iwonka Swenson told me on the telephone that she thought I would be pleased with it, so I assumed that meant I would be in it. Still, for some reason, I was nervous. My film appeared frequently throughout the documentary, but it was not identified as mine until the end of the program. Other eyewitnesses appeared in their interviews interspersed into the program. The documentary was interesting, but with only a few minutes left in the program, I had not yet appeared; but I had not yet given up hope that at least part of my interview would be included.

Finally, with less than five minutes remaining, they introduced me into the documentary. Max Holland, creator of the "lost bullet" theory, interviewed me as the limousine replica turned around us on the corner, and without being asked, I volunteered that I thought the limousine should be closer to me than it had been staged. He asked me to clarify, which I did. Then the television narrator said they were going to test my memory by looking more closely at my film to see if it showed

JFK's limousine closer to me. When they did, Mr. Holland determined that the limousine *had* been a few inches closer to the south side of the street as it turned onto Elm, which helped his theory. I know they based this documentary on a theory, but I never dreamed anything I said in my interview would end up as seemingly a key part of the investigation...after forty-eight years. I knew beforehand what the subject of this documentary was and that the theory being explored was that the first bullet had been deflected by the traffic light or traffic light mast in front of where my parents and I were standing. However, I had no idea how they would use (or even *if* they would use) anything I said in the finished documentary. I only said what I have always said—Sears Tower Varizoom 8 mm camera, Daddy took one magnificent photo of the presidential limo, three shots, firecrackers, stranger pulled me to the ground, I quit filming because I could see only the back of the limo disappearing into the crowd, and so on. But during the interview, I found myself standing in the same place I stood on November 22, 1963, and as I watched the replica of the presidential limousine turn in front of me again, something seemed off—I thought the limo seemed a little too far away from me. I don't know why I even mentioned it at the time, because it did not seem that important. Whether my remark was really that important or not, I don't know, but it was exciting for me anyway. Since that production aired, Mr. Holland amended the conclusion he made in the program, which is too technical for me to address.

    Soon after *JFK: The Lost Bullet* aired, I received a call from Dustin Blanchard with KXAN television, the local NBC affiliate in the Austin area. It was 4:30 p.m. on November 22, 2011, and Mr. Blanchard had just completed an on-camera interview with Dan Sullivan at Image Trends, Inc. Mr. Sullivan gave Mr. Blanchard my phone number, and KXAN wanted to interview me in connection with the Image Trends interview and the NatGeo TV documentary. Mr. Blanchard asked if he could interview me that evening and told me the interview would air on the early morning news the next day. I had about an hour to prepare. I rushed to put on my makeup, fix my hair, and get dressed in the little time I had to prepare. It was probably a good thing I did not have more time to think about it, because I started to get nervous. Mr. Blanchard arrived in a little over an hour. I relaxed as soon as we shook hands, and within minutes, he had his camera set up for the interview in my upstairs office. It aired the following morning, November 23, at approximately 5:45 a.m. I never have high expectations for any interviews I do, but he did a good job.

Following the Dustin Blanchard interview and as a result of his interview, on November 29, 2011, I received a call from Korri Kezar, a reporter for the local Leander Ledger in Leander, Texas, where I live. She came to the house to interview me, and her long article ran in the December 15, 2011, paper. I was pleased to do the interview, and Ms. Kezar did a good job, too. My husband Gene teased me about the fact that my picture appeared above the fold on the front page.

The year 2011 was exciting. The year 2012 has also been interesting; and I will see what 2013, leading up to the fiftieth anniversary, has in store for me and my historic images.

CHAPTER 9

Where Were You?

After I began writing my story, I asked my sisters to tell me about where they were and what they were doing when they heard the news about Kennedy's assassination. Patsy was living in Austin with her husband Bob, who was attending the University of Texas, and their three-year-old son Michael. Patsy was exhausted and sleep deprived from having a husband who stayed up all night studying and a small child, so she was trying to take advantage of some quiet time while Michael napped and Bob studied. She had her head under a pillow listening to music on the radio. The news broke into the programming, and she cried. She was not aware that President Kennedy was going to Dallas and didn't find out until much later that Mother, Dad, and I went to see the presidential motorcade. She doesn't know when she saw our photos and movie for the first time, but it could have been years after the fact.

My sister Nancy was a student at Texas Tech in Lubbock, Texas, in 1963. On the day Kennedy was assassinated, tired from studying, she was lying down in her dorm room taking an afternoon nap. She was annoyed when she awoke to the sound of someone's radio blaring down the hall. She went to the room where the noise was coming from to tell them to turn it down. As she followed the noise to its source, she began listening and couldn't believe what she was hearing. When she realized what had happened, she immediately returned to her room, put some decent clothes on, and went to the lounge where a TV was broadcasting the catastrophic news.

Nancy's future husband Larry Pennington was in the US Navy and was stationed in Bremerhaven, Germany, in 1963. He was at the bowling alley on the base when he heard the news. Later that evening he went to a pub in town named the Odeon, where he heard a merchant marine and a German woman discussing what had happened. The Germans loved President Kennedy because of his "Ich bin ein Berliner" speech at the Berlin Wall earlier in 1963. As the merchant marine and the woman talked about what happened, Larry commented to them, "I'm from Dallas." The woman slapped him across the face.

Larry also related to me via e-mail on July 9, 2003, the following:

> "The day of the assassination, my grandmother and grumpaw were in a Laundromat on 7th St. behind the Texas Theater and saw Oswald get out of a car out front and come in to make a pay phone call on a phone right above Granny's purse. She watched closely because of his proximity to her 'very valuable' coin purse right under the phone. Granny told the police later [about this] when she saw his picture on the news but they said it could not have been him and never came out to speak further with her. After the call, he went out the back door and walked 4 blocks down the alley to the Texas Theater where he was apprehended. One of the two officers that arrested him is a member of the church Nancy and I are now attending. My cousin held suicide watch over Ruby the last 30 days he lived in police custody.

[He] was an officer at the time and is now retired. The next morning after the assassination, my [mother] was on the bus going to Sangers at 5:00 am and at the [Texas School Book Depository] Warehouse location the city had lights out and several cement trucks busily filling all the drainage holes along the street curb at the assassination site."

In an e-mail to me, my friend Kaye Lotman from Oak Cliff also explained to me what it was like for her mother after the assassination:

"My mother was playing the organ at Donnell's Cafeteria in the shopping center near Stockard [Junior High] the night that JFK was assassinated. She wrote a little about it in a journal. She said, 'I remember that Monday evening after the late President J. F. Kennedy was assassinated right here in our own city. People everywhere were shocked and stunned with the news. All our hearts were full of mixed emotion, and the need of togetherness seemed greater that evening. People started coming in early (to the cafeteria), seeming to seek consolation. All our hearts were heavy, but as people gathered, we started playing and singing some patriotic songs and some religious songs. Many people told me this was the most fitting thing that could have been possible under the circumstances. We closed the evening with our wonderful patriotic song, 'God Bless America.' That evening will always remain an outstanding, memorable one for me and many others by their own testimony.'"

In an e-mail to me in November 2011, my cousin Phyllis Irwin described when she heard about the assassination.

"[November 22, 1963] was a day during my first semester as a professor here in Fresno. I was teaching a voice class when the news came down the hall from the office in the music department. Then there was this slow and silent exodus from the building and the university...few words, just some tears and shudders and emptiness feelings."

As per his oral history recorded by The Sixth Floor Museum at Dealey Plaza in 2008, in 1963 my husband Gene worked for a company who operated convenience stores in Louisiana. On the day of the assassination, he was attending a statewide tax seminar in Baton Rouge when he heard an announcement about the shooting of the president in Dallas. He said many people stood up and applauded but were later embarrassed when they found out it was not a joke. Subsequently, the meeting adjourned, and everyone went home.

Epilogue

I was born in 1950. To me, as a child and a young adult in the 1950s and 1960s, events even from the 1940s might as well have happened centuries earlier, so I think I understand why generations of people born after 1963 might feel distanced or disconnected from the assassination of John F. Kennedy. Today, when I have an opportunity to speak with people born after 1963, I usually see a general lack of interest in the assassination. Some don't know who John F. Kennedy was. Perhaps *my story* will help some people connect in some way to 1963, even if it's just by a thread. I don't blame the young people. Instead, I think the public school system as a whole does not offer students a balanced and comprehensive picture of our nation's history.

I also find it somewhat humorous when a young person (sometimes even a journalist) asks me about the "video" I took on November 22, 1963. I restrain myself from the temptation to correct the use of the word "video" with the word "film," because I have begun to think it's not important any longer.

Over the decades, when asked what I think happened on November 22, 1963, or if I thought there was a conspiracy, my answer has not changed. I heard three gunshots, which seemed equidistant apart and sounded, to my young ears, like firecrackers. I don't have a theory, conspiracy or otherwise, but I seriously doubt it would have been possible for one person to accomplish an act of such magnitude without someone else's knowing about it. That is the limit of my theory.

In the years closely following the assassination, when I occasionally met Kennedy researchers in person, I noticed a look of disbelief on their faces when they learned I was not totally consumed by the assassination. I harbored my own thoughts about them, wondering how they managed to have the time and/or resources to research the assassination. I suspect it is a hobby for some people, an obsession for some, and a vocation for a select few.

While writing this book, I closely studied a few photographs and films from November 22, 1963, showing my parents and me. I had seen these images before, but in many respects, I was seeing them for the first time. I guess it felt this way because I had a new perspective. I wasn't looking for clues to the assassination; rather, I was uncovering clues to my own past—what we were doing and how we looked. It was especially exciting to see my parents and me so clearly in the restored Elsie Dorman film.

In addition to reviewing my husband's and my oral histories recorded in 2008 by The Sixth Floor Museum at Dealey Plaza, I also reviewed the oral history the Museum recorded of my parents and me in 1996. I noticed some minor discrepancies between what I recorded in the oral histories and what I now remember. Going through my files helped make some things more clear. If anyone wonders which is more accurate, I would lean toward my book rather than the oral history. However, the differences are minor, and I do not want to diminish the relevance of the oral histories. As an example, during my oral history at the Museum in 2008, I stated that I made the last few seconds of my film, which I took to use up the remaining film on the reel, after my father returned from the grassy knoll area. While writing my book, after mentally stepping carefully through the sequence of events, I began to think I could have taken (and probably did take) that footage while my father had gone down to the grassy knoll. He could easily have been exploring the grassy knoll area with the throngs of other people for longer than fifteen minutes. Gary Mack wrote in an email to me dated August 17, 2011 that, in his opinion, little more

Epilogue

than fifteen minutes could have elapsed by the time I took that end-of-reel segment. I clearly remember Daddy asking me to do this, which I believe he would have meant for me to do while he walked down to the grassy knoll. Otherwise, he might have used up the end of the movie reel himself.

In the early years after the assassination, Daddy had custody of the slides and the film. He kept them in an old metal US Army file box, which he kept in a closet. He kept all of our other home movies in that box, too, which I still have. Our original home movies are still inside (except for the Kennedy reel); however, I had all of the Towner home movies transferred to video about twenty years ago. Mother and Daddy moved to Hamilton, Texas, in 1972. When he gave me custody of our JFK film and transparencies at that time, I stored them in a large brown envelope in *my* closet for a few years. As previously mentioned, I eventually placed them in a bank safety-deposit box; and as I moved around the Dallas area, I relocated the film and transparencies into nearby banks. After The Sixth Floor Exhibit opened to the public in 1989, I agreed to allow them to store my original images in cold storage, which is where they remain. I would be interested in knowing where other eyewitness amateur photographers stored their images over the years.

As the years fly by, I occasionally reflect on November 22, 1963 and the surrounding events. I have questions, but they aren't as much about the assassination as they are about my parents and me:

- Did Daddy wish we had been closer to the assassination or was he glad we were not? If we had moved farther down Elm like Daddy wanted to at the time, would we have been right where the president received his fatal head wound?
- Was there a higher power at work preventing us from setting up our vantage point farther down Elm toward the triple underpass? I am grateful for not being any closer to the assassination than I was. I have never wished we had been closer.
- Before the motorcade arrived, when we were waiting at the corner of Houston and Elm, was the assassin watching us? Some people

have even asked me if I thought the assassin used us as targets to practice aiming. I guess it's possible.
- What would I have done if I had looked up and actually seen a man with a gun in the Texas School Book Depository building?
- If I had panned up with my movie camera, would I have caught the image of the assassin in the sixth floor window?
- In Elsie Dorman's film, who is the man in the engineer's hat and overalls talking to Daddy right after he finished taking his photo of the presidential limousine, and what did they say to each other?
- Who pulled me down to the ground when the gunshots erupted?
- What images would I have captured if I had had more film in my camera and the presence of mind to use it?
- Did Daddy regret not having more film in the movie camera or taking more photographs, and why did I never ask him that question?
- What was Mother thinking after the assassination as she waited with me on the plaza for Daddy to come back from investigating down Elm Street and over the grassy knoll? Was she worried about him?
- Why did I go back to school after the assassination that day? Why did my parents allow me to go back to school? I should be able to answer this, but I can't, and I guess I never will.
- How bothered was Daddy that the authorities never contacted him, or was he relieved? Other than *Life* magazine in 1967, the only interview Mother and Dad did was the oral history for The Sixth Floor Museum at Dealey Plaza in 1996.
- What happened to some of the people we communicated with about the assassination: Patsy Swank (*Life 1967*); Vincent Guarino ('*Teen 1968*); Eileen from Pennsylvania, who wrote me two fan letters; and Martin J. Daly and William Brown, staff investigators for the House of Representatives Select Committee on Assassinations 1977?
- What did Mother and Dad think about their thirteen-year-old daughter witnessing such a violent, tragic, and historic event? Did they worry about my emotional well-being? If they did, it wasn't apparent. I am not being critical when I say this. I don't recall that they ever asked me if I was OK after the assassination. No one ever asked if the event traumatized me; therefore, I never felt that way. I

was OK. Today it would be so different for a student who witnessed such a tragedy. At school, students would be encouraged (if not required) to seek counseling and to think deeply about it.
- If my dad or I had captured the actual assassination on film, would he have lived to be eighty-nine, and would I be alive today? I don't think so.
- Did Daddy ever doubt my ability to use the movie camera to film the presidential motorcade? He exhibited extreme confidence in me when he asked me to film the motorcade and the grassy knoll area *after* the assassination. At the time, it seemed quite normal for him to ask me; however, in hindsight, I feel honored that he trusted me so implicitly.

Most of all, I regret that I wasn't able to begin writing this book while my parents were still living and able to talk about it. They could have answered many of my questions. Sadly, even if I had had the notion to write about my experience while my parents were alive, I would have had no time for such a project until recently, far too late to discuss it with them.

Daddy became emotional any time he tried to talk about it. I have not. Rarely does the subject bring me to tears. I can't even think of when it ever did. I guess that is because of my age at the time of the assassination. However, I frequently became emotional while watching Daddy struggle with his feelings. Maybe my time is still coming.

Still today, I rarely bring up the subject of the Kennedy assassination. If someone specifically asks me about it, I will gladly discuss it; however, when it somehow comes up in conversation with people who do not know my story, it often—quite curiously—causes an awkward silence from which the conversation does not recover. There have been many, but two such occasions stand out in my mind. It happened once in a college journalism class in San Angelo in 1969. As part of a class assignment, I read Mark Lane's *Rush to Judgment* (a book about the assassination), and I gave an oral report about it. I included some of my personal story in my report. None of the students had any questions for me at the end of my presentation, and there was no class discussion, which had followed the other students' oral reports. Were the students not interested, did they think I was boasting, was it a bad oral report, or were they simply speechless? Regardless of the reason, I was very uncomfortable.

It happened again in the 1990s. For a few months, I saw a family counselor for help in dealing with numerous issues. I didn't consider any of my problems to be insurmountable, individually, but when issues with my children arose, on the advice of a family physician, I sought counseling. As it turned out, I had many topics to discuss—divorce; raising teenagers as a single working mother; financial strain; dealing with the stress of a full-time job and a three- to four-hour daily round trip commute to work; and helping my sisters as caregivers for our aging and increasingly dependent parents. The counselor already seemed skeptical about my accurate description of my normal happy upbringing, which I compared to TV families like the Cleavers (*Leave It to Beaver*), the Nelsons (*Ozzie and Harriet*) and the Cunninghams (*Happy Days*). Once, however, during a normal course of questioning, the therapist caught me off guard by asking if there had been any traumatic events in my life. I thought for a few seconds. The Kennedy assassination was the farthest thing from my mind at the time, and I initially answered, "No," followed by, "Oh, well, I was an eyewitness to the Kennedy assassination." I followed that tidbit of information up with a brief description of the event as it pertained to me. I am sure I fumbled with the words, as I couldn't decide how to spit them out. I immediately knew it was going to be awkward, and it was. When I finally answered, the therapist was clearly taken aback. She became silent and didn't seem to know how to continue. Other than what seemed to be an obligatory follow-up question or two, such as my age at the time, she spent no further time or energy on the subject.

Again, I am not complaining—just making an observation. I have had the honor of speaking with other eyewitness photographers of the assassination who have shared with me similar conversation-halting experiences. I never received any kind of counseling on the subject, nor did my parents. I never thought it caused me any problems, and I assume my parents felt the same way. Unfortunately, the three of us

Epilogue

never discussed how it *had* affected us. I certainly wish I could have a conversation about it with them now.

One facet to writing my story is that I seriously doubt I would have written this book had it not been for the technology, resources, and online publishing opportunities the twenty-first century affords, which has definitely made my project much easier than it would have been only a few years ago. I now marvel at how much work all published authors must have gone through to get a book published, especially before electronic resources and tools became a part of our lives. The job is big enough the way I have done it—self publish. I can't imagine writing a book by hand or even typing one on an old-fashioned manual typewriter. I learned to type on a manual typewriter in high school, and I still have an old Royal manual typewriter that belonged to my parents. I brought it out of the closet to display it, and when I noticed it still had a ribbon in it, I had the bright idea it would be fun to type a letter to my sister on it. After approximately six words, I changed my mind. (For the young people reading this book, the keys on the old typewriters are hard to press, and there are limited punctuation keys, for example, no exclamation mark, which, instead, is an apostrophe+backspace+period. Making corrections was a huge problem–even minor ones, and making carbon copies was also a challenge. Typing fifty to sixty words per minute on an old typewriter was fast. Forty was good.)

It is also interesting to consider what improved technology has done for my JFK images. Initially, it was a major undertaking to copy the 8 mm film or the transparencies, and projecting the original images exposed them to wear and tear and risked damage. Duplicating the images meant either I had to release the original images into the hands of professionals or so-called professionals, or I had to babysit the original images during the duplication process, and there were few local companies I could trust to duplicate such valuable and historical images safely. Neither scenario was acceptable. Then came video, which made it easy to view my film and Daddy's transparencies once the images *were* transferred to video. The advent of digital technology made it easier still to duplicate the images. Finally, in 2011, in connection with the National Geographic TV documentary that year, Image

Trends, Inc., restored my film almost to its original state, with the assistance of National Geographic, The Sixth Floor Museum at Dealey Plaza, and The Library of Congress.

As for the actual assassination of President John Fitzgerald Kennedy, there seems to be more than the distance of time between the "me" today and the "me" on November 22, 1963. In some ways, it seems as if that skinny thirteen-year-old girl in bobby sox standing with her parents on the corner of Houston and Elm was someone else—someone I once knew.

I think my son Chris summed it up at the age of five in 1987 when he asked me, *"When someone grows up, are they the same person as they were when they were little?"* Hang on, Chris. I'm still searching for the answer to that one.

* * *

Sources

Billings, Richard N., Associate Editor, *Life*. Letter to J. M. Towner. October 11, 1967.

Brown, William. Memorandum to Clifford A. Fenton. December 8, 1977.

Cutler, R. B. *Seventy-Six Seconds in Dealey Plaza: Evidence of Conspiracy*. Massachusetts: 1978. Print.

"David Lifton." *Wikipedia.com*. August 26, 2011. Web. October 15, 2011. http://en.wikipedia.org/wiki/David_Lifton.

Hunt, George P. Managing Editor. Editor's Note: "Finding Pictures of a Moment in History." *Life,* November 24, 1967: 3. Print.

"Lee Bowers." *Wikipedia.com*. November 2, 2011. Web. November 5, 2011. http://en.wikipedia.org/wiki/Lee_Bowers.

"Nov. 22, 1963, Dallas: Photos by nine bystanders," *Life* November 24, 1967: 87-97. Print.

Mack, Gary. Email to author. May 9, 2012.

Mack, Gary. Email to author. September 26, 2012.

Montgomery, Marian Ann. Letter to author. December 18, 1996.

Pender, Eugene. Oral History with Stephen Fagin. The Sixth Floor Museum at Dealey Plaza, Dallas. February 1, 2008.

"Robert Stone Biography." *Robertstoneproductions.com*, 2012. Web. March 6, 2012. http://robertstoneproductions.com/.

Towner, James M. Interview. Photographer's Session inside Dallas County Commissioner's Court room. The Sixth Floor Museum at Dealey Plaza, Dallas. November 22, 1996.

Towner, James M., Patricia D. Towner, Tina Towner Barnes. Oral History with Bob Porter and Gary Mack. The Sixth Floor Museum at Dealey Plaza, Dallas. March 30, 1996.

Towner, Tina. Oral History with Stephen Fagin. The Sixth Floor Museum at Dealey Plaza, Dallas. February 1, 2008.

Towner, Tina. "View From the Corner." *'Teen,* June 1968, 46. Print.

Other Sources

Essays and letters written by Patricia Bailey.

Essays and letters written by Nancy Pennington.

Front cover motorcade images:
Photographed by Tina Towner, November 22, 1963
© 1983 Mary C. Barnes (Tina Barnes)
All rights reserved

Made in the USA
Lexington, KY
06 January 2013